"Pádraig Ó Tuama casts devotion as an art form that belongs to all of us, and art itself as an engine of devotion, a way to be present in the messy, complicated, divine fabric of our world."

—MOLLY McCULLY BROWN, *Places I've Taken My Body*

"Pádraig Ó Tuama offers us a month of prayers that brim with the warmth, insight, and lush description that listeners to *Poetry Unbound* have come to expect. The faithful will find themselves refreshed and renewed in these pages, and those estranged from religion will find balm and blessing."

—THE REV. JASON MYERS, *Maker of Heaven &*; editor in chief of *EcoTheo Review*

"In this slim collection of daily devotions and essays, Ó Tuama shows once again that he is not just a great poet — he is a singular theologian."

—JESSICA GOUDEAU, *After the Last Border*

"*Being Here* is a gentle, generous, and compelling spiritual companion; a book that engages the head, the heart, the whole seeking self. 'Turn our tables over,' Ó Tuama writes, 'so we can see the / spirit in the places / we are rejecting.' Because Ó Tuama believes in us, we can believe in prayer anew."

—NICK RIPATRAZONE, *The Habit of Poetry*; culture editor for *Image Journal*

being here

Prayers for Curiosity, Justice, and Love

PÁDRAIG Ó TUAMA

WILLIAM B. EERDMANS PUBLISHING COMPANY

GRAND RAPIDS, MICHIGAN

Wm. B. Eerdmans Publishing Co.
4035 Park East Court SE, Grand Rapids, Michigan 49546
www.eerdmans.com

Printed in the United States of America

30 29 28 27 26 25 24   2 3 4 5 6 7

ISBN 978-0-8028-8347-6

Library of Congress Cataloging-in-Publication Data

A catalog record for this book is available from the Library
of Congress.

Unless otherwise indicated, Scripture quotations come from
the New Revised Standard Version.

A PRAYER FOR THE PEOPLE

Turning to the light
the light turns to us.
Moving toward the source
the source moves us.
Holding on to hope
hope holds on to us.
Jesus of Nazareth,
you encountered many lives
calling people to justice
love and curiosity.
May we — in all our nights, days
and activities — act with more
justice, love and curiosity.
Because this might save us,
and make us more like you,
who turns to us in love.
Amen.

— written for the Church of the Heavenly Rest
in Manhattan, August 2020

Contents

Being Here: What Is Prayer?

SOMEWHERE, A LONG TIME AGO, a man was in distress.
He had been trying to make a point about power and
religion and community and the vocation of being
human. His friends thought he was rousing them to
war — some of them brought swords. His detractors
sought to quiet him, so they brought swords, too.
Somewhere an empire yawned, and another annoying
upstart was silenced.

Before he died, he went to a place he liked, a little
garden, near a town.

And he prayed. He was exhausted, the kind of ex-
haustion that's beyond sleep. He brought himself to his
prayer: his exhaustion, the pressure he was under, the
crisis he was facing, the possibility that he might find a
way out, the sense of abandonment that was creeping
up on him. What is prayer? Well, here it was truth.
Here it was taking a cold hard look at his world and
wondering if he could find it in himself to do anything
differently. In the face of death, he tried to find some-
thing that could help him.

What is prayer? I don't know really. But if it's any-
thing, it must be a repository for the experience of to-
day, a place for reckoning, with yourself, with the story
of God that you tell or don't tell, with the decisions
you're facing, with the guts of yourself.

He was stressed, this man. He sweated, even at
night. Blood vessels burst. What is prayer? It's a way

to live a life, it seems. Certainly that's how this man shaped it. I don't know if prayers are answered. There's a yes/no imagination that often limits the possibilities of the practice. I think of prayer as a place of encounter, a place of yearning, a place of reckoning, of discerning. I think of prayer as a favorite emptiness, a place where your aloneness is accompanied by a mystery you place your trust in. I think of prayer as the great listening. Is anyone listening? Helloooooo. Low. Oh. O. There's an echo, of desire and yearning. There's that, at least. But — for thousands and thousands of years — people have believed there's more. There is a great Nothing from which the Everything came forth. And the Nothing's listening. And we might find ourselves listening to the great listening that's listening to us. It's like a dream after waking, it's just at the edge of your senses.

During the pandemic years, I was poet in residence for the Church of the Heavenly Rest in Manhattan. In those first months I was at home in Ireland, upstairs in my little room, with books and cork tiling on the wall to stop sound bouncing round when I recorded poetry podcasts. Everybody was in little tiles on the screen. We were all in our rooms. In one room someone's bird peered at us all with a quizzical eye. In another room someone got a blanket and wrapped it around them. In another room a person made coffee. In another room someone cried. That was prayer too: feeling, comfort, rest for the weary, looking at each other, something wild looking back.

When you walk out the front doors of Church of the Heavenly Rest, you're facing Central Park. In the park there are all kinds of birds — little and large — who pay no attention to pandemics: ducks, chickadees, hawks, owls. There are mice rustling through the leaves. There are squirrels. It's thought there's a coyote. There are thousands of trees. There is a network of communication underneath the ground keeping the trees in touch with the trees. There is another city in this city. What is prayer? Well, it's looking too.

—◇—

"Manhattan" is a word that comes from the language of the Lenape people. It means, I'm told, something about a thicket where there are trees whose branches are good for making bows, bows for hunting, bows for providing. Whenever I come to this island, I touch the ground, thinking of the ground that has been the homeplace of people for thousands of years before European people arrived with limited imagination of what possession, profit, and production meant. What is prayer? It's a protest, it's a lament, it's paying that debt, it's telling the truth. It is knowing that more than one thing happened.

The prayers in this book are numbered: one, two, three, up until thirty-one. The idea is that you might pray one prayer every day of the month. You can scratch them out, replace words, write your own. They're all collects, a little fivefold form of prayer that is — for me — as important as the form of sonnet. A collect starts by naming the one it's praying to. Then it unfolds a little bit of that one. Then it names a single desire, and then it unfolds a little bit of the desire being named. It ends with an amen, a little bird of praise. What noise does that bird make? What does it see? Where is it going?

The hope is that you can turn to a prayer with the story of your life, and in the little emptiness you create there, hear something, discern something, feel something that's connecting you to other things seeking out connection with you. What is prayer? It's not a passport to heaven. If anything, it's a way of seeing here, a way of being here.

Pádraig Ó Tuama

How to Use This Book

A FEW YEARS AGO, I was speaking at an event in London. It was an event that had some connection to religion, so it began with a liturgy in the chapel. I was due to speak about poetry afterward. I sat at the back of the chapel and waited for the liturgy to begin. The organizers were nice, and so I was looking forward to hearing what words they'd chosen and arranged for public consumption. The chapel had fifty people in it, but it was small, so it felt cozy.

As things began, an order of service was handed out. Glancing at it, I saw that they'd used a lot of poems and prayers that I'd written. That was fine — I'm always curious how people make use of such things. The service went as services go. People spoke the bits in bold, or didn't, or stood, or didn't, or sang, or didn't.

I'd likely have forgotten this liturgy except for what was happening beside me. A woman, wearing a long expensive rich brown overcoat, and a silk scarf (mostly deep wine in color), fished around in her bag for a pen. Then set about redacting the liturgy. I could hear her mutter, "No, no, no," as she crossed out words from the liturgy (words I'd written) and replaced them with words she preferred. The sounds she made were much more interesting than the sounds I've heard in other liturgies. Exasperation. Infuriation. Irritation. Her order of service resembled a piece of art by the end of the twenty minutes. I was really hoping she'd leave it behind. I was about three feet away from her so couldn't quite read what she had written.

I wondered how I'd chat to her if she happened to be part of the retreat on poetry I was giving. But, alas, she wasn't part of that group. I have no idea who she was. Maybe she was the director of this retreat center. Maybe she'd wandered in accidentally.

I wonder, too, what was happening for her in the industry of her redaction and correction and amendment ("industry," from the Latin *industria*, meaning diligence). Was she bored with whatever words I'd written in collects and poems that had been arranged? Did she want them to be wilder? Did they stoke anger in her? Were they predictable and she wished them to be less so? I have no idea.

There's a text in the Codex Bezae — a fifth-century binding of the four Gospels and Acts — that is not included in the canonical Gospels. But I love it, and remember coming across it in my undergrad (the chance comment a lecturer made sent me off on a tangent for years). The Codex Bezae has this at Mark 6:4:

> On the same day, when he saw a certain man working on the Sabbath, he said to him, "Oh man, if you know what you are doing, you are blessed; but if you do not know, you are cursed, and a transgressor of the Law."

Partly the reason I like this so much is because Jesus is so annoying. Whatever anyone thinks of the claims about his divinity, he's certainly recognizable. There are scholars who say this phrase meets a number of the criteria for passing the "Did Jesus of Nazareth say this really? really really really" test, because (a) this text is found in a few places, and (b) it definitely sounds like Jesus-can't-give-a-straight-answer-Christ.

The woman in the chapel in London and the strange Jesus staring back at us from the Codex Bezae.

The man working on the Sabbath too. And you, reading this. And me. All of us. And prayer. The question for me is one of freedom. Are the words in a prayer book ones that are staid, failing, unimaginative, and confining? Cross them out. Burn them. Make a fire to build an altar to any God who's worthy of the words you have to offer. If we do this freely, then I think — I hope — we are doing wisely. But are the words feeling too risky, are they asking us to put flesh on the Jesus of Nazareth whose divinity is interrupting his tongue? Is fear the reason why certain words are avoided? This book doesn't matter (give it away; prop up that wobbly table with it). But the state of the soul is: if the language of prayer seeks anything, it seeks freedom. And fear seeks to control freedom, not focus it.

All of this is about permission. If you're not sure what to do with this book, then perhaps reading the opening prayer followed by the small texts for the day (one from a gospel tradition, the other from something more contemporary), then some silence before the collect on the day, and then the final remembering prayer might be a good shape. Certainly, it's not a bad shape for now.

But you might have tried all of that and want to try something new. Perhaps you want to start at the end and begin with remembering. Perhaps you want to write your own prayers in the margins. Perhaps you want to edit or amend mine. Maybe they need to be wilder. Maybe you want to scribble your own readings into the corners or write the dates on which you used a particular prayer in the margins.

Perhaps you want to read the gospel and reading before you take a walk and read the prayer of the day when you get back. Lovely. Perhaps you want to read the gospel text in the morning and the prayer at night. Also lovely. Perhaps you want to copy them into your phone and have them pop up as a reminder every day. Also magnificent.

Perhaps you want to read the gospel text for the day, then take ten deep breaths, read the reading for the day, followed by another ten breaths, and then the collect, finishing off with more deep breaths. I'm delighted. Or maybe you keep it by the kettle and skim through the thoughts while you've got that sixty seconds to yourself.

If you know what you're doing, you're blessed. If you don't know what you're doing, then try it one way for a month, and another way for another month, and then go with what works. You're the one who'll bless these prayers by praying them. This is how to use this book. Make it yours.

The Art and Form of the Collect:
A Craft Essay

WHEN I LEARNED THAT A SONNET was less interested in fourteen lines and more interested in its volta — its turn, its revolution, its revolver — my understanding of sonnet changed. Up until then I'd imagined that its past was more form-based than its current iterations. Suddenly, though, I realized that the past of a sonnet was more fluid and flexible than contemporary strict iterations of its form: eleven-line, thirteen-line, or even up to seventeen-line little songs, as the translation goes. Not everything about the past was flexidox though: the rhyming scheme and syllabic count of those sonnets were unquestionable until they weren't.

In the poetry traditions that have emerged out of Europe, the sonnet asks for attention. It is a small punch of a poem, sometimes looking like a clenched fist — if it's all in one burst — or two clenched fists of different sizes. It takes a topic and looks at it, with the benefit of a turn. From Shakespeare to Patience Agbabi, from John Donne to Terrence Hayes, the English-language sonnet has entered the imagination of poets, crafters of language who have something to say and choose to enter the room of a sonnet in order to say it.

Growing up, I learned other forms too, some structure-based, but others that were more thematic. In Irish-language poetry, there was a form whereby Ireland was spoken of by means of a substitute: something domestic, agricultural, everyday — a cow, for instance.

The idea was that the colonialists — if they could understand Irish, or demand a translation on pain of threat — would scoff at the rural Irish composing verses for their cattle. But the cow was Ireland. It was a poem of pride, of national protection, of language, and resistance. Form has a function in hiding, too.

Other forms were made available: the aisling is a poem where a poet falls asleep under a tree but wakes because a sky-woman, a spéirbhan, is in front of him, weeping and lamenting her lover lost at sea. Melodrama, perhaps, but also the sky-woman is Ireland, mourning France, or Spain, or whoever it is that was supposed to send an armada to aid Ireland under occupation. Form reveals and conceals, is a repository for feeling, and is a conversation back and forth through time. A speaker is more than just a speaker, a speaker might be a community, a congregation, a hope — dashed or expectant — or a lament.

While I was involved in charismatic Christianity, I was often confused. PRAY we were often told, with demand. Mostly I wandered graveyards and begged not to be hated by the God I prayed to. Eventually, mostly out of exhaustion, I started turning to the old forms I knew well. The rosary, the stations of the cross, some *lectio divina*. Those provided a container, and at least I could stop feeling like shit at the end of those mandatory times of devotion. I needed more containers, though, more forms. Ones that made space for language but also had the capacity to hold wild language. The collect presented itself.

The oldest written collect is in Latin, around one thousand years ago. But for a collect to be written implies it's older than the paper it's written on.

Deus cui omne cor patet et omnis voluntas loquitur: et quem nullum latet secretum: purifica per infusionem sancti spiritus cogitationes cordis nostri: ut te perfecte diligere et digne

laudare mereamur, per dominum nostrum ie-
sum christum filium tuum qui tecum vivit et
regnat in unitate eiusdem spiritus sancti deus,
per omnia secula seculorum. Amen.

It's a precursor to what is known as the Collect for
Purity in contemporary liturgies in the worldwide An-
glican Communion. An early English-language version
of the same collect is found in *The Cloud of Unknowing*,
a mystical text by an unknown scribe, probably written
in the late 1300s:

God, unto whom alle hertes ben open, and unto
whom alle wille spekith, and unto whom no
privé thing is hid: I beseche thee so for to clense
the entent of myn heart with the unspekable gift
of thi grace that I may parfiteliche love thee, and
worthilich preise thee. Amen.

Before looking at the structure — and it's a beauti-
ful fivefold structure — it's worthwhile thinking about
the word "collect." In liturgical circles it's pronounced
with the emphasis on the first syllable — COLLect —
rather than the ordinary usage of going to collect
a message, where the emphasis is on the second —
collECT. There's no magic about this. It's tradition,
or distinction, or dialect, or snobbery, or something
else. Call it what you want. Either way it's collecting
something; namely, your intention and desire, your re-
flection and attention, your gratitude, and your need
for containment.

The collect is a form. It is a declaration in the first
person, as well as a hope for a conversation with others
who've found room in the structure of the form. It's a
shape. And the hope is that a shape can hold. There
are old questions — in literature and theology — about
whether one can be free within a prescribed form.
But better to learn from than be restricted by those

arguments. If Elizabeth Bishop and Colette Bryce can write sestinas as perfect as they have, if Danez Smith's corona of sonnets in *Don't Call Us Dead* can do what they do, if Mary Oliver's complex, rage-and-lament-filled book-length poem *The Leaf and the Cloud* can make up its own form, and if Patricia Smith's range of page to stage works, then the old binaries of form and restriction have been proven to be limiting in their imagination.

The collect has five folds:

1. Name the one you're praying to
2. Unfold the name of the one you're praying to
3. Name one desire
4. Unfold the desire you've named
5. Finish with a bird of praise

1. God,
2. unto whom alle hertes ben open, and unto whom alle wille spekith, and unto whom no privé thing is hid:
3. I beseche thee so for to clense the entent of myn heart with the unspekable gift of thi grace
4. that I may parfiteliche love thee, and worthilich preise thee.
5. Amen.

Basically, it's:

1. Address
2. Say more
3. Ask one thing
4. Say more
5. End

As a form, it's elegant, asking for attention to the second and fourth folds, "Say more." Why are you praying to the one you're praying to? Who are they anyway? Why are you asking for the single thing you're asking for? What's the heart of that desire?

I've taught this collect form in many groups: clergy, poets, young people, fiction writers, retreatants, agnostics, devout. For each, the form issues a call. To the devout, they may find themselves suddenly wishing to address a collect to a character like Pilate. "Am I praying to a despot?" they may ask, and it's less about the despot and more about the direction. They may be uncomfortable addressing a prayer to anyone other than their God.

Another person, a fiction writer, say, may write a collect to their minor character in their story and suddenly find a long conversation emerging through an ancient form meant for prayer. Someone else may write a collect to someone who has died, or someone may find themselves addressing God in the name of their favorite phenomenon in nature. "Glorious Sunrise," someone said once, and someone objected, saying it wasn't good enough. "Lord" is pretty weak, if you ask me, coming from a colonized country. Every utterance of language is a failure; nothing encompasses everything it can mean. The question is how our language — in poetry or prayer — can fail in new ways.

If a prayer is to have meaning for a public audience, then it needs to manage some complicated things with elegance. A collect can't be too long. It needs some space. It needs to make life recognizable, and somehow conjugate a life into the pronouns it employs for its purpose. I always like choosing a text — from one gospel or another — as a conversation piece with a collect. In a way, a collect is shaped within the form of a dialogue. It's a fragmentary response to a fragmentary excerpt. Isn't that the truth though? Everything's a bit of everything. There's no pressure to make language comprehensive. To imagine that language can say everything might mean that it says nothing. It can speak from the particular. And that particular may have a wider audience than we think.

Why a bird of praise? Why not? I suppose technically you could call it a laudatory doxology, but who can be bothered? I like birds. I like the idea that a collect — a small form that names what the writer hopes the future might unfold has, within it, a small moment of pause, to imagine an animal, something utterly present to its instinct and need, guided by hunger. And in that moment, the prey and praise of praying all echo. We are consumed and we consume. We live and we live with death. We ask, knowing that nothing will finally satiate what death will demand of us. What to do then? Consider birds.

At a conference, a young person was leading prayers. It was a gathering of all kinds of people: agnostic, atheist, devout, ex-religious, fairly liberal, nostalgic for the religion of childhood. The young person was practicing hospitality. "God, or Buddha, or the Divine, or the Universe, or the Source of All, or the Ground of Being, or the Essence, is among us," he started off by saying. And then he said, "Each of us, as we know, has our own approach to God, or Buddha, or the Divine, or the Universe, or the Source of All, or the Ground of Being, or the Essence."

It went on like this. A drop-down menu of options for whatever worked. His kindness and desire to include were exceptional. And exhausting. The prayer, meant to be about a minute long, was already far longer than it should be, and we seemed nowhere near the end. "Son," someone said at one point, eighty years old to the young man's eighteen, "Would you just say *something*?" It was an appeal for brevity, an appeal for particularity, an appeal to trust the fact that those who were listening could do their own discerning, translating, redacting, or transposing. It was also an appeal for form. Something that reveals and conceals, a repository for feeling in the skeleton of simple language.

DAILY PRAYERS

day 1

OPENING PRAYER

Turning to the day
and to each other

> We open ourselves to the day
> and each other.

This is the day that the Lord has made
and a day we'll have to make our way through.

> Whether with ease or pain
> with patience or joy

May we find opportunities for generosity
toward others and ourselves.

> May we find moments of encounter
> even in isolation.

May we find stories and memories
even in the most complicated corners.

> May we start again
> where we have failed again.

May we confess
and be confessed to.

> Because this is a way of living
> That's worth living daily.

"Làpìch knewël."   *I will see you again.*
— Lenape farewell

And Salmon the father of Boaz by Rahab, and Boaz the father of Obed by Ruth, and Obed the father of Jesse, and Jesse the father of King David. And David was the father of Solomon by the wife of Uriah.
— Matthew 1:5–6   *day 1*

COLLECT OF THE DAY

Grandmothers of Jesus,
In your stories we hear of your
courage and creativity,
your tenacity,
and the things you faced down.
Here, today, we stand in the time after you
and look back,
with gratitude for stories like yours
that help us live today.

Help us live today
in all the stories of our lives
so that we can stand in your great
ache and wash.
Amen.

A REMEMBERING PRAYER

God of day and night,
In the great poem of creation
we read that we
were considered very good,
and that you
find glory
in us.

We look around our city:
the birds finding home
the name of it
the shape of it
the bustle and magnificence of it

day 1

the poverty of it
the complicity of it
the repressed stories of it

the generosity of it
the corners of kindness
on every corner

the future of it
the past it hides from
greed and goodness
violence and visions
burdens and bodies
everywhere.

We pray for our city
and for the cities we are.

Breathe in us
just like you always do
and renew us
with every twilight
with every morning
with every encounter
with every opportunity.

day 2

Turning to the day
and to each other

> We open ourselves to the day
> and each other.

This is the day that the Lord has made
and a day we'll have to make our way through.

> Whether with ease or pain
> with patience or joy

May we find opportunities for generosity
toward others and ourselves.

> May we find moments of encounter
> even in isolation.

May we find stories and memories
even in the most complicated corners.

> May we start again
> where we have failed again.

May we confess
and be confessed to.

> Because this is a way of living
> That's worth living daily.

Why does one feel so different at night? Why is it so exciting to be awake when everybody else is asleep? Late — it is very late! And yet every moment you feel more and more wakeful, as though you were slowly, almost with every breath, waking up into a new, wonderful, far more thrilling and exciting world than the daylight one. And what is this queer sensation that you're a conspirator? Lightly, stealthily you move about your room. You take something off the dressing-table and put it down again without a sound. And everything, even the bedpost, knows you, responds, shares your secret. . . .

day 2

You're not very fond of your room by day. You never think about it. You're in and out, the door opens and slams, the cupboard creaks. You sit down on the side of your bed, change your shoes and dash out again. A dive down to the glass, two pins in your hair, powder your nose and off again. But now — it's suddenly dear to you. It's a darling little funny room. It's yours. Oh, what a joy it is to own things! Mine — my own!"

— Katherine Mansfield, "At the Bay"

When Elizabeth heard Mary's greeting, the child leaped in her womb. And Elizabeth was filled with the Holy Spirit and exclaimed with a loud cry, "Blessed are you among women, and blessed is the fruit of your womb."

— Luke 1:41–42

SILENCE

COLLECT OF THE DAY

day 2   Walls of Elizabeth's room,
You, too, heard the cries of delight
when two judged women
found shelter in each other.
May all our rooms
be rooms where people can speak
from the deepest joy of them,
the deepest need,
the deepest trust,
and the deepest truth.
Because these rooms
are blessed.
Amen.

A REMEMBERING PRAYER

God of day and night,
In the great poem of creation
we read that we
were considered very good,
and that you
find glory
in us.

We look around our city:
the birds finding home
the name of it
the shape of it
the bustle and magnificence of it

the poverty of it
the complicity of it
the repressed stories of it

the generosity of it
the corners of kindness
on every corner

the future of it
the past it hides from
greed and goodness
violence and visions
burdens and bodies
everywhere.

We pray for our city
and for the cities we are.

Breathe in us
just like you always do
and renew us
with every twilight
with every morning
with every encounter
with every opportunity.

day 2

day 3

Turning to the day
and to each other

> We open ourselves to the day
> and each other.

This is the day that the Lord has made
and a day we'll have to make our way through.

> Whether with ease or pain
> with patience or joy

May we find opportunities for generosity
toward others and ourselves.

> May we find moments of encounter
> even in isolation.

May we find stories and memories
even in the most complicated corners.

> May we start again
> where we have failed again.

May we confess
and be confessed to.

> Because this is a way of living
> That's worth living daily.

Dust as we are, the immortal spirit grows
Like harmony in music; there is a dark
Inscrutable workmanship that reconciles
Discordant elements, makes them cling together
In one society. How strange that all
The terrors, pains, and early miseries,
Regrets, vexations, lassitudes interfused
Within my mind, should e'er have borne a part,
And that a needful part, in making up
The calm existence that is mine when I   *day 3*
Am worthy of myself! Praise to the end!
Thanks to the means which Nature deigned to
    employ;
Whether her fearless visitings, or those
That came with soft alarm, like hurtless light
Opening the peaceful clouds; or she may use
Severer interventions, ministry
More palpable, as best might suit her aim.

— William Wordsworth, from *The Prelude*

Her husband Joseph, being a righteous man and unwill-
ing to expose her to public disgrace, planned to dismiss
her quietly. But just when he had resolved to do this,
an angel of the Lord appeared to him in a dream.

— Matthew 1:19–20

SILENCE

COLLECT OF THE DAY

day 3   Joseph, man of dreams,
In your dreams you were willing
to let your righteousness
be made even more right.
What you thought was good
wasn't good enough
and you changed course.
In our decisions help us listen
to the dreams that know better,
that go deeper, that push through.
Because we need to know better,
go deeper,
push through.
Amen.

A REMEMBERING PRAYER

God of day and night,
In the great poem of creation
we read that we
were considered very good,
and that you
find glory
in us.

We look around our city:
the birds finding home
the name of it
the shape of it
the bustle and magnificence of it

the poverty of it
the complicity of it
the repressed stories of it

the generosity of it
the corners of kindness
on every corner

the future of it
the past it hides from
greed and goodness
violence and visions
burdens and bodies
everywhere.

We pray for our city
and for the cities we are.

Breathe in us
just like you always do
and renew us
with every twilight
with every morning
with every encounter
with every opportunity.

day 4

Turning to the day
and to each other

> We open ourselves to the day
> and each other.

This is the day that the Lord has made
and a day we'll have to make our way through.

> Whether with ease or pain
> with patience or joy

May we find opportunities for generosity
toward others and ourselves.

> May we find moments of encounter
> even in isolation.

May we find stories and memories
even in the most complicated corners.

> May we start again
> where we have failed again.

May we confess
and be confessed to.

> Because this is a way of living
> That's worth living daily.

To a Brown Boy

'Tis a noble gift to be brown, all brown,
  Like the strongest things that make up this
    earth,
Like the mountains grave and grand,
  Even like the very land,
  Even like the trunks of trees —
  Even oaks, to be like these!
God builds His strength in bronze.

day 4

To be brown like thrush and lark!
  Like the subtle wren so dark!
Nay, the king of beasts wears brown;
  Eagles are of this same hue.
I thank God, then, I am brown.
  Brown has mighty things to do.

— Effie Lee Newsome, "The Bronze Legacy"

SCRIPTURE

While they were there, the time came for her to deliver her child. And she gave birth to her firstborn son and wrapped him in bands of cloth, and laid him in a manger, because there was no place for them in the *kataluma* [upper room].

— Luke 2:6–7

SILENCE

day 4

Householders of Bethlehem,
When your upper room was full
you welcomed unknown kin in
to your living room: your floor;
your beds; your mangers full of
hay, the place where your born
children had been warmed.
No nasty innkeeper, just houses
crammed with people keeping
empire at bay. No rejection, just
ordinary hospitality.
In all our hospitalities, help us
give and take. May exchanges be
warmed by hearts open to change.
Because this is how a God made
a home among a people. Because
this is how a people make homes
around a newborn God.
Amen.

A REMEMBERING PRAYER

God of day and night,
In the great poem of creation
we read that we
were considered very good,
and that you
find glory
in us.

We look around our city:
the birds finding home
the name of it
the shape of it
the bustle and magnificence of it

the poverty of it
the complicity of it
the repressed stories of it

the generosity of it
the corners of kindness
on every corner

the future of it
the past it hides from
greed and goodness
violence and visions
burdens and bodies
everywhere.

We pray for our city
and for the cities we are.

Breathe in us
just like you always do
and renew us
with every twilight
with every morning
with every encounter
with every opportunity.

day 5

Turning to the day
and to each other

> We open ourselves to the day
> and each other.

This is the day that the Lord has made
and a day we'll have to make our way through.

> Whether with ease or pain
> with patience or joy

May we find opportunities for generosity
toward others and ourselves.

> May we find moments of encounter
> even in isolation.

May we find stories and memories
even in the most complicated corners.

> May we start again
> where we have failed again.

May we confess
and be confessed to.

> Because this is a way of living
> That's worth living daily.

Tiger, tiger, burning bright
In the forests of the night,
What immortal hand or eye
Could frame thy fearful symmetry?

In what distant deeps or skies
Burnt the fire of thine eyes?
On what wings dare he aspire?
What the hand dare seize the fire?

day 5

And what shoulder and what art
Could twist the sinews of thy heart?
And, when thy heart began to beat,
What dread hand and what dread feet?

What the hammer? what the chain?
In what furnace was thy brain?
What the anvil? what dread grasp
Dare its deadly terrors clasp?

When the stars threw down their spears,
And watered heaven with their tears,
Did He smile His work to see?
Did He who made the lamb make thee?

Tiger, tiger, burning bright
In the forests of the night,
What immortal hand or eye
Dare frame thy fearful symmetry?

— William Blake, "The Tiger"

SCRIPTURE

He was in the wilderness forty days, tempted by Satan;
and he was with the wild beasts; and the angels waited
on him.

— Mark 1:13

SILENCE

'

COLLECT OF THE DAY

day 5 Jesus of the animals,
When you faced the end
 — even at the start —
you found friends in
unexpected places. Animals
with warm hearts and fur,
strange tastes and needs
and habits.
When we are at the end,
meet us in the touch of
beasts uninterested in
grand designs.
Because in your own emptiness
you knew what you needed,
and you found it claw, and fur,
and teeth, and pointed ears.
Amen.

A REMEMBERING PRAYER

God of day and night,
In the great poem of creation
we read that we
were considered very good,
and that you
find glory
in us.

We look around our city:
the birds finding home
the name of it
the shape of it
the bustle and magnificence of it

day 5

the poverty of it
the complicity of it
the repressed stories of it

the generosity of it
the corners of kindness
on every corner

the future of it
the past it hides from
greed and goodness
violence and visions
burdens and bodies
everywhere.

We pray for our city
and for the cities we are.

Breathe in us
just like you always do
and renew us
with every twilight
with every morning
with every encounter
with every opportunity.

day 6

Turning to the day
and to each other

> We open ourselves to the day
> and each other.

This is the day that the Lord has made
and a day we'll have to make our way through.

> Whether with ease or pain
> with patience or joy

May we find opportunities for generosity
toward others and ourselves.

> May we find moments of encounter
> even in isolation.

May we find stories and memories
even in the most complicated corners.

> May we start again
> where we have failed again.

May we confess
and be confessed to.

> Because this is a way of living
> That's worth living daily.

Sweet hours have perished here;
   This is a mighty room;
Within its precincts hopes have played, —
   Now shadows in the tomb.

           — Emily Dickinson, XXV ("Sweet Hours")

SCRIPTURE

When he returned to Capernaum after some days, it *day 6* was reported that he was at home. So many gathered around that there was no longer room for them, not even in front of the door; and he was speaking the word to them.

           — Mark 2:1–2

SILENCE

Homely Jesus,
Your friends knew where you lived
and called around
when you came back,
with casserole and curiosity,
with pressure and with
sensitivity.
When our friends come back
help us help them with anything

day 6

that'd help them, leaving
what won't work outside,
bringing what will work inside.
So that we can hear them
and everything they say.
Amen.

A REMEMBERING PRAYER

God of day and night,
In the great poem of creation
we read that we
were considered very good,
and that you
find glory
in us.

We look around our city:
the birds finding home
the name of it
the shape of it
the bustle and magnificence of it

the poverty of it
the complicity of it
the repressed stories of it

the generosity of it
the corners of kindness
on every corner

the future of it
the past it hides from
greed and goodness
violence and visions
burdens and bodies
everywhere.

We pray for our city
and for the cities we are.

Breathe in us
just like you always do
and renew us
with every twilight
with every morning
with every encounter
with every opportunity.

day 7

OPENING PRAYER

Turning to the day
and to each other

> We open ourselves to the day
> and each other.

This is the day that the Lord has made
and a day we'll have to make our way through.

> Whether with ease or pain
> with patience or joy

May we find opportunities for generosity
toward others and ourselves.

> May we find moments of encounter
> even in isolation.

May we find stories and memories
even in the most complicated corners.

> May we start again
> where we have failed again.

May we confess
and be confessed to.

> Because this is a way of living
> That's worth living daily.

READING

I felt as if aided from above. My tongue was cut loose, the stammerer spoke freely; the love of God, and of his service, burned with a vehement flame within me — his name was glorified among the people.

— Jarena Lee, *Religious Experience and Journal of Mrs. Jarena Lee*

SCRIPTURE

A Samaritan woman came to draw water.

day 7

— John 4:7

SILENCE

COLLECT OF THE DAY

Jesus of Nazareth,
Who was it that taught you
the art of conversation?
You explored your own edges
as you invited others to explore theirs.
In choice and conversation, may we
find delight in the sharp edges of each other.
Because this woman did, and we remember her.
Amen.

day 7

A REMEMBERING PRAYER

God of day and night,
In the great poem of creation
we read that we
were considered very good,
and that you
find glory
in us.

We look around our city:
the birds finding home
the name of it
the shape of it
the bustle and magnificence of it

the poverty of it
the complicity of it
the repressed stories of it

the generosity of it
the corners of kindness
on every corner

the future of it
the past it hides from
greed and goodness
violence and visions
burdens and bodies
everywhere.

We pray for our city
and for the cities we are.

Breathe in us
just like you always do
and renew us
with every twilight
with every morning
with every encounter
with every opportunity.

day 8

Turning to the day
and to each other

> We open ourselves to the day
> and each other.

This is the day that the Lord has made
and a day we'll have to make our way through.

> Whether with ease or pain
> with patience or joy

May we find opportunities for generosity
toward others and ourselves.

> May we find moments of encounter
> even in isolation.

May we find stories and memories
even in the most complicated corners.

> May we start again
> where we have failed again.

May we confess
and be confessed to.

> Because this is a way of living
> That's worth living daily.

We take a moment to be quiet. Remember that we are not here on our own. That we are surrounded by a cloud of witnesses. We welcome into this company our bright and benevolent. Our wise and well Ancestors who have dreamed of these days for us. And so, as we breathe in, we remember that our lives are filled with their hopes, with their love and with their dreams. As we breathe out, we know that we can't live up to their expectations. But we know that we are also surrounded by the presence of God who is love and as we breathe in, we receive God's love, into every cell of our body. And as we breathe out, we breathe everything that no longer serves love. And so, as we breathe in, we receive all of and as much of God's love as we need. And as we breathe out. We let go of everything else that doesn't serve us and doesn't serve love.

day 8

> — Bishop Vincentia Kgabe,
> daily prayer from ordination retreat

SCRIPTURE

Jesus says: "Blessed is the person who has struggled. They have found life."

> — Gospel of Thomas (58)

SILENCE

Jesus of the struggle,
You never promised ease:
yours the pained heart; ours the pained hearts too.
You promised life in the hustle and bustle
of the everyday.
Meet us in this tussle
so that we may find energy
to keep going.
Meet us with rest too. You needed it;

day 8   we do too.
Amen.

A REMEMBERING PRAYER

God of day and night,
In the great poem of creation
we read that we
were considered very good,
and that you
find glory
in us.

We look around our city:
the birds finding home
the name of it
the shape of it
the bustle and magnificence of it

the poverty of it
the complicity of it
the repressed stories of it

the generosity of it
the corners of kindness
on every corner

the future of it
the past it hides from
greed and goodness
violence and visions
burdens and bodies
everywhere.

We pray for our city
and for the cities we are.

Breathe in us
just like you always do
and renew us
with every twilight
with every morning
with every encounter
with every opportunity.

day 9

Turning to the day
and to each other

> We open ourselves to the day
> and each other.

This is the day that the Lord has made
and a day we'll have to make our way through.

> Whether with ease or pain
> with patience or joy

May we find opportunities for generosity
toward others and ourselves.

> May we find moments of encounter
> even in isolation.

May we find stories and memories
even in the most complicated corners.

> May we start again
> where we have failed again.

May we confess
and be confessed to.

> Because this is a way of living
> That's worth living daily.

READING

A table means more than a glass even a looking glass
is tall. A table means necessary places and a revision
a revision of a little thing it means it does mean that
there has been a stand, a stand where it did shake.

— Gertrude Stein, *Tender Buttons*

SCRIPTURE

day 9

And as he sat at dinner in Levi's house, many tax col-
lectors and sinners were also sitting with Jesus and his
disciples — for there were many who followed him.
When the scribes of the Pharisees saw that he was
eating with sinners and tax collectors, they said to his
disciples, "Why does he eat with tax collectors and sin-
ners?" When Jesus heard this, he said to them, "Those
who are well have no need of a physician, but those
who are sick; I have come to call not the righteous
but sinners."

— Mark 2:15–17

SILENCE

Jesus at the table,
which one are you? The one asking for
the bread, or the one passing salt?
The one listening, or laughing,
or asking awkward questions?
Every table is a possibility of encounter.
Help us make it so,
with questions and answers, with
listening and change,

day 9

with food and drink,
with love and soup and invitation.
Amen.

A REMEMBERING PRAYER

God of day and night,
In the great poem of creation
we read that we
were considered very good,
and that you
find glory
in us.

We look around our city:
the birds finding home
the name of it
the shape of it
the bustle and magnificence of it

the poverty of it
the complicity of it
the repressed stories of it

the generosity of it
the corners of kindness
on every corner

the future of it
the past it hides from
greed and goodness
violence and visions
burdens and bodies
everywhere.

We pray for our city
and for the cities we are.

Breathe in us
just like you always do
and renew us
with every twilight
with every morning
with every encounter
with every opportunity.

day 10

Turning to the day
and to each other

> We open ourselves to the day
> and each other.

This is the day that the Lord has made
and a day we'll have to make our way through.

> Whether with ease or pain
> with patience or joy

May we find opportunities for generosity
toward others and ourselves.

> May we find moments of encounter
> even in isolation.

May we find stories and memories
even in the most complicated corners.

> May we start again
> where we have failed again.

May we confess
and be confessed to.

> Because this is a way of living
> That's worth living daily.

READING

I early accustomed myself to look for the hand of God
in the minutest occurrence and to learn from it a les-
son of morality and religion; and in this light every
circumstance I have related was to me of importance.
After all, what makes any event important, unless by
its observation we become better and wiser, and learn
"to do justly, to love mercy, and to walk humbly be-
fore God"? To those who are possessed of this spirit,
there is scarcely any book or incident so trifling that
does not afford some profit, while to others the expe-
rience of ages seems of no use; and even to pour out to
them the treasures of wisdom is throwing the jewels of
instruction away.

> — Olaudah Equiano,
> *The Interesting Narrative of the Life of*
> *Olaudah Equiano, or Gustavus Vassa,*
> *the African Written By Himself*

SCRIPTURE

On that day, when evening had come, he said to them,
"Let us go across to the other side." And leaving the
crowd behind, they took him with them in the boat,
just as he was. Other boats were with him.

> — Mark 4:35–36

SILENCE

Jesus of the horizon,
you were always looking
toward other boats,
other shores, other stories.
As we're shaped by your story,
help us remember other stories too:
making their own way
to the shore, just as they are,
like, and not like, you.

day 10   Amen.

A REMEMBERING PRAYER

God of day and night,
In the great poem of creation
we read that we
were considered very good,
and that you
find glory
in us.

We look around our city:
the birds finding home
the name of it
the shape of it
the bustle and magnificence of it

day 10

the poverty of it
the complicity of it
the repressed stories of it

the generosity of it
the corners of kindness
on every corner

the future of it
the past it hides from
greed and goodness
violence and visions
burdens and bodies
everywhere.

We pray for our city
and for the cities we are.

Breathe in us
just like you always do
and renew us
with every twilight
with every morning
with every encounter
with every opportunity.

day 11

Turning to the day
and to each other

> We open ourselves to the day
> and each other.

This is the day that the Lord has made
and a day we'll have to make our way through.

> Whether with ease or pain
> with patience or joy

May we find opportunities for generosity
toward others and ourselves.

> May we find moments of encounter
> even in isolation.

May we find stories and memories
even in the most complicated corners.

> May we start again
> where we have failed again.

May we confess
and be confessed to.

> Because this is a way of living
> That's worth living daily.

Pip saw the multitudinous, God-omnipresent, coral insects, that out of the firmament of waters heaved the colossal orbs. He saw God's foot upon the treadle of the loom, and spoke it; and therefore his shipmates called him mad. So man's insanity is heaven's sense; and wandering from all mortal reason, man comes at last to that celestial thought, which, to reason, is absurd and frantic.

— Herman Melville, *Moby Dick*

day 11

SCRIPTURE

When they had rowed about three or four miles, they saw Jesus walking on the sea and coming near the boat, and they were terrified. But he said to them, "It is I; do not be afraid." Then they wanted to take him into the boat, and immediately the boat reached the land toward which they were going.

— John 6:19–21

SILENCE

COLLECT OF THE DAY

Jesus of frustrations,
So much interrupts us:
the deadline, the storm, the old hatred,
the unhealed wound, the barrier.
Help us follow life
in the midst of everything that comes.
Introduce yourself to us
in these strange places,
because we seek destinations.

day 11   Amen.

A REMEMBERING PRAYER

God of day and night,
In the great poem of creation
we read that we
were considered very good,
and that you
find glory
in us.

We look around our city:
the birds finding home
the name of it
the shape of it
the bustle and magnificence of it

the poverty of it
the complicity of it
the repressed stories of it

the generosity of it
the corners of kindness
on every corner

the future of it
the past it hides from
greed and goodness
violence and visions
burdens and bodies
everywhere.

We pray for our city
and for the cities we are.

Breathe in us
just like you always do
and renew us
with every twilight
with every morning
with every encounter
with every opportunity.

day 12

Turning to the day
and to each other

> We open ourselves to the day
> and each other.

This is the day that the Lord has made
and a day we'll have to make our way through.

> Whether with ease or pain
> with patience or joy

May we find opportunities for generosity
toward others and ourselves.

> May we find moments of encounter
> even in isolation.

May we find stories and memories
even in the most complicated corners.

> May we start again
> where we have failed again.

May we confess
and be confessed to.

> Because this is a way of living
> That's worth living daily.

I sat and talked with you
In the shifting fire and gloom,
Making you answer due
In delicate speech and smooth —
Nor did I fail to note
The black curve of your head
And the golden skin of your throat
On the cushion's golden-red.
But all the while, behind,
In the workshop of my mind,
The weird weaver of doom
Was walking to and fro,
Drawing thread upon thread
With resolute fingers slow
Of the things you did not say
And thought I did not know,
Of the things you said to-day
And had said long ago,
To weave on a wondrous loom,
In dim colours enough,
A curious, stubborn stuff —
The web that we call truth.

day 12

— Dorothy Sayers, "Sympathy"

People were bringing even infants to him that he might
touch them; and when the disciples saw it, they sternly
ordered them not to do it.

— Luke 18:15

SILENCE

COLLECT OF THE DAY

Jesus of welcome,
you, too, suffered
under the restrictions
of self-appointed policing.
Your friends, believing
they understood you,
misunderstood what you meant
by welcome.
Us, too.
May we hear your rebukes.
Because, unless we do,
our belonging betrays us.
Amen.

A REMEMBERING PRAYER

God of day and night,
In the great poem of creation
we read that we
were considered very good,
and that you
find glory
in us.

We look around our city:
the birds finding home
the name of it
the shape of it
the bustle and magnificence of it

the poverty of it
the complicity of it
the repressed stories of it

the generosity of it
the corners of kindness
on every corner

the future of it
the past it hides from
greed and goodness
violence and visions
burdens and bodies
everywhere.

We pray for our city
and for the cities we are.

Breathe in us
just like you always do
and renew us
with every twilight
with every morning
with every encounter
with every opportunity.

day 12

day 13

Turning to the day
and to each other

> We open ourselves to the day
> and each other.

This is the day that the Lord has made
and a day we'll have to make our way through.

> Whether with ease or pain
> with patience or joy

May we find opportunities for generosity
toward others and ourselves.

> May we find moments of encounter
> even in isolation.

May we find stories and memories
even in the most complicated corners.

> May we start again
> where we have failed again.

May we confess
and be confessed to.

> Because this is a way of living
> That's worth living daily.

What shall we render unto the Lord for them? Sacrifices and burnt offerings are no longer pleasing to him: the pomp of public worship, and the ceremonies of a festive day, will find no acceptance with him, unless they are accompanied with actions that correspond with them.

— Absalom Jones, "A Thanksgiving Sermon"

day 13

A person said to him, "Tell my brothers to divide my father's possessions with me." He said to him, "Oh man, who has made me a divider?"

— Gospel of Thomas (72)

COLLECT OF THE DAY

Distant Jesus,
You are often hard to grasp.
Help us see where we break the things
we say we wish to save
so that we might imagine
a different kind of being in this world together.
Amen.

day 13

A REMEMBERING PRAYER

God of day and night,
In the great poem of creation
we read that we
were considered very good,
and that you
find glory
in us.

We look around our city:
the birds finding home
the name of it
the shape of it
the bustle and magnificence of it

the poverty of it
the complicity of it
the repressed stories of it

the generosity of it
the corners of kindness
on every corner

the future of it
the past it hides from
greed and goodness
violence and visions
burdens and bodies
everywhere.

We pray for our city
and for the cities we are.

Breathe in us
just like you always do
and renew us
with every twilight
with every morning
with every encounter
with every opportunity.

day 14

Turning to the day
and to each other

> We open ourselves to the day
> and each other.

This is the day that the Lord has made
and a day we'll have to make our way through.

> Whether with ease or pain
> with patience or joy

May we find opportunities for generosity
toward others and ourselves.

> May we find moments of encounter
> even in isolation.

May we find stories and memories
even in the most complicated corners.

> May we start again
> where we have failed again.

May we confess
and be confessed to.

> Because this is a way of living
> That's worth living daily.

Long have I known a glory in it all,
But never knew I this;
Here such a passion is
As stretcheth me apart, — Lord, I do fear
Thou'st made the world too beautiful this year;
My soul is all but out of me, — let fall
No burning leaf; prithee, let no bird call.

> — Edna St. Vincent Millay, "God's World"

day 14

SCRIPTURE

"Are not two sparrows sold for a penny? Yet not one of them will fall to the ground apart from your Father. And even the hairs of your head are all counted. So do not be afraid; you are of more value than many sparrows."

> — Matthew 10:29–31

SILENCE

COLLECT OF THE DAY

Jesus of the beasts,
you noticed foxes, birds, cattle, sheep;
fish, and humans too.
Looking at other breathing things,
even trees,
may we see our place in this fragile family,
because unless we do
we'll subdue them,
demeaning the value

day 14   of everything that lives
or moves
or has being.
Amen.

A REMEMBERING PRAYER

God of day and night,
In the great poem of creation
we read that we
were considered very good,
and that you
find glory
in us.

We look around our city:
the birds finding home
the name of it
the shape of it
the bustle and magnificence of it

the poverty of it
the complicity of it
the repressed stories of it

the generosity of it
the corners of kindness
on every corner

the future of it
the past it hides from
greed and goodness
violence and visions
burdens and bodies
everywhere.

We pray for our city
and for the cities we are.

Breathe in us
just like you always do
and renew us
with every twilight
with every morning
with every encounter
with every opportunity.

day 15

Turning to the day
and to each other

> We open ourselves to the day
> and each other.

This is the day that the Lord has made
and a day we'll have to make our way through.

> Whether with ease or pain
> with patience or joy

May we find opportunities for generosity
toward others and ourselves.

> May we find moments of encounter
> even in isolation.

May we find stories and memories
even in the most complicated corners.

> May we start again
> where we have failed again.

May we confess
and be confessed to.

> Because this is a way of living
> That's worth living daily.

READING

The great scene of grief, in which the wild infant bore
a part, had developed all her sympathies; and as her
tears fell upon her father's cheek, they were the pledge
that she would grow up amid human joy and sorrow,
nor forever do battle with the world, but be a woman
in it.

— Nathaniel Hawthorne, *The Scarlet Letter*

SCRIPTURE

"For where two or three are gathered in my name,
I am there among them." Then Peter came and said
to him, "Lord, if another member of the church sins
against me, how often should I forgive? As many as
seven times?"

— Matthew 18:20–21

SILENCE

COLLECT OF THE DAY

We disinvite the unkind from our tables,
unfriend them, unfollow them,
oftentimes for good reason.
Whatever the reason,
may we be safe enough — eventually —
to consider
wishing well for them
even if they stray far
from the ways that could help them.

day 15   Amen.

A REMEMBERING PRAYER

God of day and night,
In the great poem of creation
we read that we
were considered very good,
and that you
find glory
in us.

We look around our city:
the birds finding home
the name of it
the shape of it
the bustle and magnificence of it

the poverty of it
the complicity of it
the repressed stories of it

the generosity of it
the corners of kindness
on every corner

the future of it
the past it hides from
greed and goodness
violence and visions
burdens and bodies
everywhere.

We pray for our city
and for the cities we are.

Breathe in us
just like you always do
and renew us
with every twilight
with every morning
with every encounter
with every opportunity.

day 16

Turning to the day
and to each other

> We open ourselves to the day
> and each other.

This is the day that the Lord has made
and a day we'll have to make our way through.

> Whether with ease or pain
> with patience or joy

May we find opportunities for generosity
toward others and ourselves.

> May we find moments of encounter
> even in isolation.

May we find stories and memories
even in the most complicated corners.

> May we start again
> where we have failed again.

May we confess
and be confessed to.

> Because this is a way of living
> That's worth living daily.

READING

I feel safe in the midst of my enemies; for the truth is all powerful and will prevail.

— Sojourner Truth

SCRIPTURE

A centurion there had a slave whom he valued highly, and who was ill and close to death. When he heard about Jesus, he sent some Jewish elders to him, asking him to come and heal his slave. When they came to Jesus, they appealed to him earnestly, saying, "He is worthy of having you do this for him, for he loves our people, and it is he who built our synagogue for us."

— Luke 7:2–5

day 16

SILENCE

COLLECT OF THE DAY

Unnamed Centurion of Rome,
you remind us that enemies don't come
in convenient packages.
Through the generous words of an occupied
    people
we see the story of you in new ways.
We hope you saw yourself in new ways too,
through the unmerited generosity given you.
Dismantle, we pray, yourself and your empire,
as we dismantle our work and our ways.
Amen.

day 16

A REMEMBERING PRAYER

God of day and night,
In the great poem of creation
we read that we
were considered very good,
and that you
find glory
in us.

We look around our city:
the birds finding home
the name of it
the shape of it
the bustle and magnificence of it

day 16

the poverty of it
the complicity of it
the repressed stories of it

the generosity of it
the corners of kindness
on every corner

the future of it
the past it hides from
greed and goodness
violence and visions
burdens and bodies
everywhere.

We pray for our city
and for the cities we are.

Breathe in us
just like you always do
and renew us
with every twilight
with every morning
with every encounter
with every opportunity.

day 17

Turning to the day
and to each other

> We open ourselves to the day
> and each other.

This is the day that the Lord has made
and a day we'll have to make our way through.

> Whether with ease or pain
> with patience or joy

May we find opportunities for generosity
toward others and ourselves.

> May we find moments of encounter
> even in isolation.

May we find stories and memories
even in the most complicated corners.

> May we start again
> where we have failed again.

May we confess
and be confessed to.

> Because this is a way of living
> That's worth living daily.

READING

Family likeness has often a deep sadness in it. Nature, that great tragic dramatist, knits us together by bone and muscle, and divides us by the subtler web of our brains; blends yearning and repulsion; and ties us by our heart-strings to the beings that jar us at every movement.

— George Eliot, *Adam Bede*

SCRIPTURE

Now as they went on their way, he entered a certain village, where a woman named Martha welcomed him into her home. She had a sister named Mary.

— Luke 10:38–39

SILENCE

Interrupting Jesus, you found welcome
in households of tension.
In all of the tensions of our households
may we recognize the many ways
of kindness,
those on the surface
and those far below.
Because where two or three are gathered
there are more than two or three ideas.

day 17   Amen.

A REMEMBERING PRAYER

God of day and night,
In the great poem of creation
we read that we
were considered very good,
and that you
find glory
in us.

We look around our city:
the birds finding home
the name of it
the shape of it
the bustle and magnificence of it

the poverty of it
the complicity of it
the repressed stories of it

the generosity of it
the corners of kindness
on every corner

the future of it
the past it hides from
greed and goodness
violence and visions
burdens and bodies
everywhere.

We pray for our city
and for the cities we are.

Breathe in us
just like you always do
and renew us
with every twilight
with every morning
with every encounter
with every opportunity.

day 18

Turning to the day
and to each other

> We open ourselves to the day
> and each other.

This is the day that the Lord has made
and a day we'll have to make our way through.

> Whether with ease or pain
> with patience or joy

May we find opportunities for generosity
toward others and ourselves.

> May we find moments of encounter
> even in isolation.

May we find stories and memories
even in the most complicated corners.

> May we start again
> where we have failed again.

May we confess
and be confessed to.

> Because this is a way of living
> That's worth living daily.

READING

But wholly, at last, I wakened, opened wide
The window and my soul, and let the airs
And out-door sights sweep gradual gospels in,
Regenerating what I was. O Life,
How oft we throw it off and think, — 'Enough,
Enough of life in so much! — here's a cause
For rupture; — herein we must break with Life,
Or be ourselves unworthy; here we are wronged,
Maimed, spoiled for aspiration: farewell Life!'
— And so, as froward babes, we hide our eyes
And think all ended. — Then, Life calls to us
In some transformed, apocryphal, new voice,
Above us, or below us, or around. . . .

— Elizabeth Barrett Browning, *Aurora Leigh*

SCRIPTURE

Jesus stood still and called them, saying, "What do you
want me to do for you?"

— Matthew 20:32

SILENCE

Questioning Jesus,
we do not always know what we want.
Yet what we want
can drive us
even when we do not know it.
Help us find the moments to come into contact
with those deep drives
so that we can be moved
toward what will

day 18   create
and not destroy.
Amen.

A REMEMBERING PRAYER

God of day and night,
In the great poem of creation
we read that we
were considered very good,
and that you
find glory
in us.

We look around our city:
the birds finding home
the name of it
the shape of it
the bustle and magnificence of it

day 18

the poverty of it
the complicity of it
the repressed stories of it

the generosity of it
the corners of kindness
on every corner

the future of it
the past it hides from
greed and goodness
violence and visions
burdens and bodies
everywhere.

We pray for our city
and for the cities we are.

Breathe in us
just like you always do
and renew us
with every twilight
with every morning
with every encounter
with every opportunity.

day 19

Turning to the day
and to each other

> We open ourselves to the day
> and each other.

This is the day that the Lord has made
and a day we'll have to make our way through.

> Whether with ease or pain
> with patience or joy

May we find opportunities for generosity
toward others and ourselves.

> May we find moments of encounter
> even in isolation.

May we find stories and memories
even in the most complicated corners.

> May we start again
> where we have failed again.

May we confess
and be confessed to.

> Because this is a way of living
> That's worth living daily.

READING

How unwise had the wanderers been, who had deserted its shelter, entangled themselves in the web of society, and entered on what men of the world call "life," — that labyrinth of evil, that scheme of mutual torture. To live, according to this sense of the word, we must not only observe and learn, we must also feel; we must not be mere spectators of action, we must act; we must not describe, but be subjects of description.

— Mary Shelley, *The Last Man*

day 19

SCRIPTURE

"Now his elder son was in the field; and when he came and approached the house, he heard music and dancing. He called one of the slaves and asked what was going on. He replied, 'Your brother has come, and your father has killed the fatted calf, because he has got him back safe and sound.'" Then he became angry and refused to go in.

— Luke 15:25–28

SILENCE

Elder brother in the field,
when your sibling came back
no one told you. You
were left to work
and not invited to the party.
We understand your pain.
We hope you do too.
In all of our experiences of missing out
in the moments when our fears of rejection
are confirmed,
be a friend to us
inviting us to rewrite
the ending
of a story that isn't ended.
Amen.

day 19

A REMEMBERING PRAYER

God of day and night,
In the great poem of creation
we read that we
were considered very good,
and that you
find glory
in us.

We look around our city:
the birds finding home
the name of it
the shape of it
the bustle and magnificence of it

the poverty of it
the complicity of it
the repressed stories of it

the generosity of it
the corners of kindness
on every corner

the future of it
the past it hides from
greed and goodness
violence and visions
burdens and bodies
everywhere.

We pray for our city
and for the cities we are.

Breathe in us
just like you always do
and renew us
with every twilight
with every morning
with every encounter
with every opportunity.

day 20

Turning to the day
and to each other

    We open ourselves to the day
    and each other.

This is the day that the Lord has made
and a day we'll have to make our way through.

    Whether with ease or pain
    with patience or joy

May we find opportunities for generosity
toward others and ourselves.

    May we find moments of encounter
    even in isolation.

May we find stories and memories
even in the most complicated corners.

    May we start again
    where we have failed again.

May we confess
and be confessed to.

    Because this is a way of living
    That's worth living daily.

READING

I have been tables overturned, coins poured out, animals driven out of a temple, cords made into a whip. I have been found & found out.

— Sandra Montes

SCRIPTURE

The Passover of the Jews was near, and Jesus went up to Jerusalem. In the temple he found people selling cattle, sheep, and doves, and the money changers seated at their tables. Making a whip of cords, he drove all of them out of the temple, both the sheep and the cattle. He also poured out the coins of the money changers and overturned their tables.

— John 2:13–15

SILENCE

Furious Jesus,
where we have turned
places of spirit
into places of
profit
turn our tables over.
Help us see the
wreck
we are creating.

day 20 Prairielands, oceans, space
and air and woodlands.
Turn our tables over,
so we can see the
spirit in the places
we are suffocating.
Amen.

A REMEMBERING PRAYER

God of day and night,
In the great poem of creation
we read that we
were considered very good,
and that you
find glory
in us.

We look around our city:
the birds finding home
the name of it
the shape of it
the bustle and magnificence of it

the poverty of it
the complicity of it
the repressed stories of it

the generosity of it
the corners of kindness
on every corner

the future of it
the past it hides from
greed and goodness
violence and visions
burdens and bodies
everywhere.

We pray for our city
and for the cities we are.

Breathe in us
just like you always do
and renew us
with every twilight
with every morning
with every encounter
with every opportunity.

day 21

Turning to the day
and to each other

>   We open ourselves to the day
>   and each other.

This is the day that the Lord has made
and a day we'll have to make our way through.

>   Whether with ease or pain
>   with patience or joy

May we find opportunities for generosity
toward others and ourselves.

>   May we find moments of encounter
>   even in isolation.

May we find stories and memories
even in the most complicated corners.

>   May we start again
>   where we have failed again.

May we confess
and be confessed to.

>   Because this is a way of living
>   That's worth living daily.

READING

But that's always the way; it don't make no difference whether you do right or wrong, a person's conscience ain't got no sense, and just goes for him anyway. . . . It takes up more room than all the rest of a person's insides, and yet ain't no good, nohow.

— Mark Twain, *Adventures of Huckleberry Finn*

SCRIPTURE

day 21

Though Herod wanted to put him to death, he feared the crowd, because they regarded him as a prophet. But when Herod's birthday came, the daughter of Herodias danced before the company, and she pleased Herod so much that he promised on oath to grant her whatever she might ask.

— Matthew 14:5–7

SILENCE

COLLECT OF THE DAY

Scheming Herod,
you knew what you wanted to do
yet knew that if you did it
you'd suffer,
so you manipulated someone younger
to facilitate your desire.
History does not honor you,
it judges you.
May we see our actions today more clearly,

day 21   so that we are not forcing others to do
what we fear — yet want — to do.
Cast us from our petty thrones, O God of Mary.
Because we are entertaining evil
with games like this.
Amen.

A REMEMBERING PRAYER

God of day and night,
In the great poem of creation
we read that we
were considered very good,
and that you
find glory
in us.

We look around our city:
the birds finding home
the name of it
the shape of it
the bustle and magnificence of it

the poverty of it
the complicity of it
the repressed stories of it

the generosity of it
the corners of kindness
on every corner

the future of it
the past it hides from
greed and goodness
violence and visions
burdens and bodies
everywhere.

We pray for our city
and for the cities we are.

Breathe in us
just like you always do
and renew us
with every twilight
with every morning
with every encounter
with every opportunity.

day 22

Turning to the day
and to each other

> We open ourselves to the day
> and each other.

This is the day that the Lord has made
and a day we'll have to make our way through.

> Whether with ease or pain
> with patience or joy

May we find opportunities for generosity
toward others and ourselves.

> May we find moments of encounter
> even in isolation.

May we find stories and memories
even in the most complicated corners.

> May we start again
> where we have failed again.

May we confess
and be confessed to.

> Because this is a way of living
> That's worth living daily.

READING

Why are thy senses unsated
Ever in quest of elusive
    Love that is deathless?

                    — Sappho

SCRIPTURE

"I give you a new commandment, that you love one
another. Just as I have loved you, you also should love
one another. By this everyone will know that you are
my disciples, if you have love for one another."

                    — John 13:34–35

day 22

SILENCE

COLLECT OF THE DAY

Beloved Jesus,
it's said that by the end
of your favorite apostle's life
all he could whisper
was love.
Love, he said,
as his own disciples carried him to prayer.
If this is the distillation
of a life lived trying to follow you, then
day 22   help us distill.
Because there is so much noise.
Amen.

A REMEMBERING PRAYER

God of day and night,
In the great poem of creation
we read that we
were considered very good,
and that you
find glory
in us.

We look around our city:
the birds finding home
the name of it
the shape of it
the bustle and magnificence of it

the poverty of it
the complicity of it
the repressed stories of it

the generosity of it
the corners of kindness
on every corner

the future of it
the past it hides from
greed and goodness
violence and visions
burdens and bodies
everywhere.

We pray for our city
and for the cities we are.

Breathe in us
just like you always do
and renew us
with every twilight
with every morning
with every encounter
with every opportunity.

day 23

Turning to the day
and to each other

> We open ourselves to the day
> and each other.

This is the day that the Lord has made
and a day we'll have to make our way through.

> Whether with ease or pain
> with patience or joy

May we find opportunities for generosity
toward others and ourselves.

> May we find moments of encounter
> even in isolation.

May we find stories and memories
even in the most complicated corners.

> May we start again
> where we have failed again.

May we confess
and be confessed to.

> Because this is a way of living
> That's worth living daily.

Then a woman said, Speak to us of Joy and Sorrow.

And he answered:

Your joy is your sorrow unmasked.

And the selfsame well from which your laughter rises was oftentimes filled with your tears.

And how else can it be?

The deeper that sorrow carves into your being, the more joy you can contain.

Is not the cup that holds your wine the very cup that was burned in the potter's oven?

day 23

And is not the lute that soothes your spirit, the very wood that was hollowed with knives?

When you are joyous, look deep into your heart and you shall find it is only that which has given you sorrow that is giving you joy.

When you are sorrowful look again in your heart, and you shall see that in truth you are weeping for that which has been your delight.

Some of you say, "Joy is greater than sorrow," and others say, "Nay, sorrow is the greater."

But I say unto you, they are inseparable.

Together they come, and when one sits alone with you at your board, remember that the other is asleep upon your bed.

Verily you are suspended like scales between your sorrow and your joy.

Only when you are empty are you at standstill and balanced.

When the treasure-keeper lifts you to weigh his gold and his silver, needs must your joy or your sorrow rise or fall.

— Kahlil Gibran, *The Prophet*

Jesus wept.

— John 11:35

day 23

COLLECT OF THE DAY

Weeping Jesus,
friend of Mary, Martha
and their dead brother
Lazarus.
You wept when you were about to do
what you knew
would get you killed.
And you did it anyway.
Be with everyone
making tough decisions.
Because maybe there's
a way through.
Amen.

A REMEMBERING PRAYER

God of day and night,
In the great poem of creation
we read that we
were considered very good,
and that you
find glory
in us.

We look around our city:
the birds finding home
the name of it
the shape of it
the bustle and magnificence of it

the poverty of it
the complicity of it
the repressed stories of it

the generosity of it
the corners of kindness
on every corner

the future of it
the past it hides from
greed and goodness
violence and visions
burdens and bodies
everywhere.

We pray for our city
and for the cities we are.

Breathe in us
just like you always do
and renew us
with every twilight
with every morning
with every encounter
with every opportunity.

day 24

Turning to the day
and to each other

> We open ourselves to the day
> and each other.

This is the day that the Lord has made
and a day we'll have to make our way through.

> Whether with ease or pain
> with patience or joy

May we find opportunities for generosity
toward others and ourselves.

> May we find moments of encounter
> even in isolation.

May we find stories and memories
even in the most complicated corners.

> May we start again
> where we have failed again.

May we confess
and be confessed to.

> Because this is a way of living
> That's worth living daily.

It is a long held human habit to give the most atten-
tion and the best treatment to those who "fit the mold."
Their path to success and acceptance is smoother and
easier than most. But Jesus gave his attention to those
on the margins, whom society had rejected or looked
down on: women living in a man's world, despised Sa-
maritan neighbors from across the border, people who
were outcast because of illness or deformity, or who
just failed to "fit in."

day 24

Those who don't fit the norms can struggle to flour-
ish, doing work that seems designed for someone else,
frustrated or bewildered on the edge of life while the
world seems to keep turning without them. But some-
times, a kind of defiant joy can enter in, along with
a determination to live life anyway. This is what hap-
pened to people who encountered Jesus two millennia
ago — and what can happen to us too.

Whenever we feel shut out or shut down, Jesus can
fill us with this kind of defiant joy and unexpected de-
termination. And, living in the Spirit of God, we also
have the capacity to "be Christ" to one another: lifting
one another up, and transforming each other's experi-
ence from rejection to rejoicing.

— Reverend Professor Maggi Dawn

SCRIPTURE

"Listen," he said to them, "when you have entered
the city, a man carrying a jar of water will meet you;
follow him into the house he enters and say to the
owner of the house, 'The teacher asks you, "Where is
the guest room, where I may eat the Passover with my
disciples?"' He will show you a large room upstairs,
already furnished."

— Luke 22:10–12

SILENCE

COLLECT OF THE DAY

day 24   The day before you died
you told your friends
to follow the man
doing the work usually assigned
to a woman.
In such ways you knew that life
flourished
even under threat.
May we all follow those
who are truly themselves,
so that we might be
better selves
together.
Amen.

A REMEMBERING PRAYER

God of day and night,
In the great poem of creation
we read that we
were considered very good,
and that you
find glory
in us.

We look around our city:
the birds finding home
the name of it
the shape of it
the bustle and magnificence of it

day 24

the poverty of it
the complicity of it
the repressed stories of it

the generosity of it
the corners of kindness
on every corner

the future of it
the past it hides from
greed and goodness
violence and visions
burdens and bodies
everywhere.

We pray for our city
and for the cities we are.

Breathe in us
just like you always do
and renew us
with every twilight
with every morning
with every encounter
with every opportunity.

day 25

Turning to the day
and to each other

> We open ourselves to the day
> and each other.

This is the day that the Lord has made
and a day we'll have to make our way through.

> Whether with ease or pain
> with patience or joy

May we find opportunities for generosity
toward others and ourselves.

> May we find moments of encounter
> even in isolation.

May we find stories and memories
even in the most complicated corners.

> May we start again
> where we have failed again.

May we confess
and be confessed to.

> Because this is a way of living
> That's worth living daily.

READING

Wilt thou forgive that sin which I have won
    Others to sin, and made my sin their door?
Wilt thou forgive that sin which I did shun
    A year or two, but wallow'd in, a score?
        When thou hast done, thou hast not done,
          For I have more.

       — John Donne, "A Hymn to God the Father"

SCRIPTURE

As they led him away, they seized a man, Simon of Cyrene, who was coming from the country, and they laid the cross on him, and made him carry it behind Jesus.

       — Luke 23:26

SILENCE

Jesus of the Cross,
We pray for all
whose crosses
are too heavy.
Because yours was
and ours are too.
Help us bear up.
Make those who burden us
stop burdening us
day 25   so much.
Amen.

A REMEMBERING PRAYER

God of day and night,
In the great poem of creation
we read that we
were considered very good,
and that you
find glory
in us.

We look around our city:
the birds finding home
the name of it
the shape of it
the bustle and magnificence of it

the poverty of it
the complicity of it
the repressed stories of it

the generosity of it
the corners of kindness
on every corner

the future of it
the past it hides from
greed and goodness
violence and visions
burdens and bodies
everywhere.

We pray for our city
and for the cities we are.

Breathe in us
just like you always do
and renew us
with every twilight
with every morning
with every encounter
with every opportunity.

day 26

Turning to the day
and to each other

> We open ourselves to the day
> and each other.

This is the day that the Lord has made
and a day we'll have to make our way through.

> Whether with ease or pain
> with patience or joy

May we find opportunities for generosity
toward others and ourselves.

> May we find moments of encounter
> even in isolation.

May we find stories and memories
even in the most complicated corners.

> May we start again
> where we have failed again.

May we confess
and be confessed to.

> Because this is a way of living
> That's worth living daily.

READING

We want again & again in fresh words & from the new impetus & standpoint of new days the vision that sweeps ahead, the tones that fill us with faith & joy in our present share of life & work — prophetic of the splendid issues.

— Anne Gilchrist, letter to Walt Whitman

SCRIPTURE

day 26

"I have said nothing in secret. Why do you ask me? Ask those who heard what I said to them; they know what I said." When he had said this, one of the police standing nearby struck Jesus on the face, saying, "Is that how you answer the high priest?" Jesus answered, "If I have spoken wrongly, testify to the wrong. But if I have spoken rightly, why do you strike me?"

— John 18:20–23

SILENCE

COLLECT OF THE DAY

Jesus,
when the man
struck your face
you asked him a
question
of integrity.
Help all of us
in situations of
stress
day 26   to ask direct
questions.
Because you did.
And while it
didn't save you,
it kept you
close to
your own
beautiful heart.
Amen.

A REMEMBERING PRAYER

God of day and night,
In the great poem of creation
we read that we
were considered very good,
and that you
find glory
in us.

We look around our city:
the birds finding home
the name of it
the shape of it
the bustle and magnificence of it

the poverty of it
the complicity of it
the repressed stories of it

the generosity of it
the corners of kindness
on every corner

the future of it
the past it hides from
greed and goodness
violence and visions
burdens and bodies
everywhere.

We pray for our city
and for the cities we are.

Breathe in us
just like you always do
and renew us
with every twilight
with every morning
with every encounter
with every opportunity.

day 27

Turning to the day
and to each other

> We open ourselves to the day
> and each other.

This is the day that the Lord has made
and a day we'll have to make our way through.

> Whether with ease or pain
> with patience or joy

May we find opportunities for generosity
toward others and ourselves.

> May we find moments of encounter
> even in isolation.

May we find stories and memories
even in the most complicated corners.

> May we start again
> where we have failed again.

May we confess
and be confessed to.

> Because this is a way of living
> That's worth living daily.

READING

Too late loved I Thee, O Thou Beauty of ancient
days, yet ever new! too late I loved Thee! And behold,
Thou wert within, and I abroad, and there I searched
for Thee; deformed I, plunging amid those fair forms
which Thou hadst made. Thou wert with me, but I was
not with Thee. Things held me far from Thee, which,
unless they were in Thee, were not at all. Thou calledst,
and shoutedst, and burstest my deafness. Thou
flashedst, shonest, and scatteredst my blindness. Thou
breathedst odours, and I drew in breath and panted for
Thee. I tasted, and hunger and thirst. Thou touchedst
me, and I burned for Thy peace.

— Saint Augustine, *The Confessions of Saint Augustine*

SCRIPTURE

It was now about noon, and darkness came over the
whole land until three in the afternoon, while the sun's
light failed; and the curtain of the temple was torn
in two.

— Luke 23:44–45

SILENCE

Son of the Sky,
even the light failed
when you died.
And the curtain
tore itself in two:
a temple in mourning
for its child of promise.
May we mourn
with those who mourn,

day 27

letting evening come,
letting the rips and tears
be felt.
Because in mourning
we show that we have
our share in love's losses too.
Amen.

A REMEMBERING PRAYER

God of day and night,
In the great poem of creation
we read that we
were considered very good,
and that you
find glory
in us.

We look around our city:
the birds finding home
the name of it
the shape of it
the bustle and magnificence of it

the poverty of it
the complicity of it
the repressed stories of it

the generosity of it
the corners of kindness
on every corner

the future of it
the past it hides from
greed and goodness
violence and visions
burdens and bodies
everywhere.

We pray for our city
and for the cities we are.

Breathe in us
just like you always do
and renew us
with every twilight
with every morning
with every encounter
with every opportunity.

day 28

Turning to the day
and to each other

> We open ourselves to the day
> and each other.

This is the day that the Lord has made
and a day we'll have to make our way through.

> Whether with ease or pain
> with patience or joy

May we find opportunities for generosity
toward others and ourselves.

> May we find moments of encounter
> even in isolation.

May we find stories and memories
even in the most complicated corners.

> May we start again
> where we have failed again.

May we confess
and be confessed to.

> Because this is a way of living
> That's worth living daily.

I have always loved the fact that Mary Magdalene was the first person to see the resurrected Christ. She was the one who was entrusted with telling the disciples, "I have seen the Lord." This made Mary the very first Christian preacher and evangelist. Indeed, the early church gave her a special title: "apostola apostolorum," which means "apostle to the apostles."

And, from a sacramental perspective, I like to think of Mary Magdalene as the very first priest. Just as priests touch the Body of Christ at the consecration of the Eucharist (something that will occur later in our mass), Mary was the first person to touch the body of the risen Christ. We know this because Jesus says to her in today's gospel: "Do not hold on to me." Jesus tells her instead to go and to spread the Good News to his disciples. And she does exactly that.

Mary Magdalene tells the disciples: "I have seen the Lord." Five simple words that sum up the entirety of Christian belief and teaching. "I have seen the Lord." Like Mary, each of us is called to testify how our lives have been transformed by our encounter with the risen Christ. Nothing more and nothing less.

— Reverend Dr. Patrick S. Cheng, Easter sermon

day 28

Jesus said to her, "Mary!" She turned and said to him in Hebrew, "Rabbouni!"

— John 20:16

SILENCE

COLLECT OF THE DAY

Mary of Magdala,
In your grief you heard your name
and in your name
you recognized
someone who had always seen you.
We do not know you
as much as we would like.
But we ask you
to focus our eyes
on what gives life.
Because we remember you
who remembered your friend
even at the end.
Amen.

A REMEMBERING PRAYER

God of day and night,
In the great poem of creation
we read that we
were considered very good,
and that you
find glory
in us.

We look around our city:
the birds finding home
the name of it
the shape of it
the bustle and magnificence of it

the poverty of it
the complicity of it
the repressed stories of it

the generosity of it
the corners of kindness
on every corner

the future of it
the past it hides from
greed and goodness
violence and visions
burdens and bodies
everywhere.

We pray for our city
and for the cities we are.

Breathe in us
just like you always do
and renew us
with every twilight
with every morning
with every encounter
with every opportunity.

day 29

Turning to the day
and to each other

> We open ourselves to the day
> and each other.

This is the day that the Lord has made
and a day we'll have to make our way through.

> Whether with ease or pain
> with patience or joy

May we find opportunities for generosity
toward others and ourselves.

> May we find moments of encounter
> even in isolation.

May we find stories and memories
even in the most complicated corners.

> May we start again
> where we have failed again.

May we confess
and be confessed to.

> Because this is a way of living
> That's worth living daily.

As he proceeded in his work, he continued his familiar conversation with his Maker, — imploring His grace, and offering to Him all his actions.

When he had finished, he examined himself how he had discharged his duty; if he found well, he returned thanks to GOD; if otherwise, he asked pardon; and without being discouraged, he set his mind right again, and continued his exercise of the presence of GOD, as if he had never deviated from it. "Thus," said he, "by rising after my falls, and by frequently renewed acts of faith and love, I am come to a state wherein it would be as difficult for me not to think of GOD as it was at first to accustom myself to it."

day 29

As brother Lawrence had found such an advantage in walking in the presence of GOD, it was natural for him to recommend it earnestly to others; but his example was a stronger inducement than any arguments he could propose. His very countenance was edifying, such a sweet and calm devotion appearing in it as could not but affect the beholders. And it was observed that in the greatest hurry of business in the kitchen, he still preserved his recollection and heavenly-mindedness. He was never hasty nor loitering, but did each thing in its season, with an even, uninterrupted composure and tranquility of spirit. "The time of business," said he, "does not with me differ from the time of prayer; and in the noise and clatter of my kitchen, while several persons are at the same time calling for different things, I possess GOD in as great tranquility as if I were upon my knees at the blessed sacrament."

— Brother Lawrence,
The Practice of the Presence of God

When they had gone ashore, they saw a charcoal fire there, with fish on it, and bread. Jesus said to them, "Bring some of the fish that you have just caught."

— John 21:9–10

SILENCE

day 29

COLLECT OF THE DAY

Kitchen Jesus,
you surprise us
with questions
when we least expect it.
A smell returns a memory,
and there you are,
offering food and
penetrating questions.
Help us sense you,
in all the senses,
and help us hear ourselves.
Because this is where
we'll meet you.
Living though you died.
Dying though you lived.
Forever and ever.
Over and over.
Here and there.
Amen.

A REMEMBERING PRAYER

God of day and night,
In the great poem of creation
we read that we
were considered very good,
and that you
find glory
in us.

We look around our city:
the birds finding home
the name of it
the shape of it
the bustle and magnificence of it

day 29

the poverty of it
the complicity of it
the repressed stories of it

the generosity of it
the corners of kindness
on every corner

the future of it
the past it hides from
greed and goodness
violence and visions
burdens and bodies
everywhere.

We pray for our city
and for the cities we are.

Breathe in us
just like you always do
and renew us
with every twilight
with every morning
with every encounter
with every opportunity.

day 30

OPENING PRAYER

Turning to the day
and to each other

> We open ourselves to the day
> and each other.

This is the day that the Lord has made
and a day we'll have to make our way through.

> Whether with ease or pain
> with patience or joy

May we find opportunities for generosity
toward others and ourselves.

> May we find moments of encounter
> even in isolation.

May we find stories and memories
even in the most complicated corners.

> May we start again
> where we have failed again.

May we confess
and be confessed to.

> Because this is a way of living
> That's worth living daily.

There is nothing, however, misty or uncertain about what we can touch. Through the sense of touch I know the faces of friends, the illimitable variety of straight and curved lines, all surfaces, the exuberance of the soil, the delicate shapes of flowers, the noble forms of trees, and the range of mighty winds. Besides objects, surfaces, and atmospherical changes, I perceive countless vibrations. I derive much knowledge of everyday matter from the jars and jolts which are to be felt everywhere in the house.

— Helen Keller, "The Power of Touch"

SCRIPTURE

Peter said to Mary, "Sister, we know that the Saviour loved you more than the other women. Tell us the words of the Saviour that you remember, which you know and we do not, since we did not hear them." Mary replied, "What is hidden from you I will tell you."

— Gospel according to Mary 10–11

SILENCE

COLLECT OF THE DAY

Wise Mary,
You were the first to the scene
of the resurrection,
the first to witness
what we still struggle to witness
 — you saw
what was hidden.
Help us live
and hold this
day 30 hidden heart of things
inside us,
giving us life
even though we cannot
grasp it,
bringing us together
from isolation
to community.
Amen.

A REMEMBERING PRAYER

God of day and night,
In the great poem of creation
we read that we
were considered very good,
and that you
find glory
in us.

We look around our city:
the birds finding home
the name of it
the shape of it
the bustle and magnificence of it

the poverty of it
the complicity of it
the repressed stories of it

the generosity of it
the corners of kindness
on every corner

the future of it
the past it hides from
greed and goodness
violence and visions
burdens and bodies
everywhere.

We pray for our city
and for the cities we are.

Breathe in us
just like you always do
and renew us
with every twilight
with every morning
with every encounter
with every opportunity.

day 31

OPENING PRAYER

Turning to the day
and to each other

    We open ourselves to the day
    and each other.

This is the day that the Lord has made
and a day we'll have to make our way through.

    Whether with ease or pain
    with patience or joy

May we find opportunities for generosity
toward others and ourselves.

    May we find moments of encounter
    even in isolation.

May we find stories and memories
even in the most complicated corners.

    May we start again
    where we have failed again.

May we confess
and be confessed to.

    Because this is a way of living
    That's worth living daily.

What merely living clod, what captive thing,
Could up toward God through all its darkness
   grope,
And find within its deadened heart to sing
These songs of sorrow, love and faith, and hope?
How did it catch that subtle undertone,
That note in music heard not with the ears?
How sound the elusive reed so seldom blown,
Which stirs the soul or melts the heart to tears. . . .

day 31

You sang far better than you knew; the songs
That for your listeners' hungry hearts sufficed
Still live, — but more than this to you belongs:
You sang a race from wood and stone to Christ.

— James Weldon Johnson,
"O Black and Unknown Bards"

SCRIPTURE

Jesus says: "I am the light that is over all. I am the All.
The All came forth out of me. And to me the All has
come. Split a piece of wood — I am there. Lift the stone,
and you will find me there."

— Gospel of Thomas (77)

SILENCE

Jesus of the earth,
If we take these words,
we could see resurrection everywhere:
in the flight of a bird,
in a spark, in the splash of a pebble
thrown by a child,
in the sharing of a meal around a table,
in the table.
Oh let us see in such ways,

day 31   so that we might follow life
all around us.
We need this, because
in the choice between
the living and the dead,
we sometimes choose the dead.
And we need to find ways to choose
what keeps us living.
Amen.

A REMEMBERING PRAYER

God of day and night,
In the great poem of creation
we read that we
were considered very good,
and that you
find glory
in us.

We look around our city:
the birds finding home
the name of it
the shape of it
the bustle and magnificence of it

day 31

the poverty of it
the complicity of it
the repressed stories of it

the generosity of it
the corners of kindness
on every corner

the future of it
the past it hides from
greed and goodness
violence and visions
burdens and bodies
everywhere.

We pray for our city
and for the cities we are.

Breathe in us
just like you always do
and renew us
with every twilight
with every morning
with every encounter
with every opportunity.

OCCASIONAL
ESSAYS AND POEMS

Jesus in Isolation:
On the Company of Stories

AFTER A YEAR AND A HALF OF COVID, I felt like I was used to the routines. But one day, something happened. I was getting out of bed, and suddenly the world began to spin. I was no stranger to lightheadedness, but this was different. The actual house had been taken up and was going round in circles. I was in a tornado. I fell back into the bed, grasped the headboard, and began shouting for help.

What was wrong? The world was ending. I was falling, and nauseous, and frightened. It came out of nowhere. When I phoned the doctor an hour later, he said that it sounded like an ordinary but serious case of vertigo. It's a shock, he said, but there's nothing wrong; you'll throw up a lot today, and it'll take a while to clear. This felt like a metaphor I didn't want. The world was in chaos because of COVID-19, and I didn't need my brain to give me poetic devices for feeling like solid ground was shifting underneath my feet.

The doctor was right. I threw up a lot that day, and the days afterward. And it took a while to clear: the first few weeks were dicey, and then the first few months too. I relocated temporarily to New York during that time and for months still had the feeling you get when the plane begins to descend.

For the first few weeks I could barely do anything. Standing was tough. Reading was next to impossible. Watching television was an automatic stomachclencher. Light hurt. I lay on my back in a dark room with a facecloth over my eyes, felt like a damned fool and felt in need of company. I'd recently heard that my favorite book — *A Suitable Boy* by Vikram Seth, the longest single-volume novel in the English language — had been recorded, unabridged, for an audiobook. Seventy-two glorious hours narrated brilliantly by Sagar Arya. The book is populated with people I greet like old friends when they appear on the page, or in the ears. It is full of gossip, politics, flowers, saris, independence, postpartition negotiations, economic woes, melodrama, violence, friendship, affection.

I say all of this because I think that literature is a form of company. I needed something that I could listen to and be absorbed by — and troubled by, too — without the burden of wondering, Who is this character? or What just happened? I needed something that had the easy familiarity of a staircase, one I'd ascended and descended many times, so that on this ascent — dizzy, bad-metaphor-and-vertigo-laden — I might be able to stop and take it as easy as needed. The vertigo gave a particular punch too: I could only listen. Mostly with my eyes closed, lying as flat and as unmoving as was possible. Deep breathing. In the dark. The language was a companion.

When Jesus of Nazareth went into the desert of isolation, he, too, seemed to be in need of literary companionship. He'd brought nothing but himself along with him for company, but — as we all know — each self is a set of selves. So, he was in the wilderness with himselves, a possession of incarnations.

The Christian Bible includes four books commonly called the Gospels, "gospel" meaning "good news." Each account — Matthew, Mark, Luke, and John — is a window into the purpose and events of the life of Jesus of Nazareth. They vary. They tell stories in different ways. They were written for different audiences, with different agendas. Matthew, Mark, and Luke's Gospels situate Jesus's venture to the hinterlands early on in their stories of Jesus's life. Jesus has been introduced but hasn't yet launched into his public life full-tilt. What is this? Some kind of test? Or crisis? Or hazing? Or self-questioning?

The benefit of literature is that it might be all of those, or none, or some, depending on the person reading. The text itself has a certain flow of its own logic, but that is only ever one way of reading. We are read as we read. And the stories that matter become a part of us. *A Suitable Boy* is one of a few books (see also *Pride and Prejudice, Lord of the Rings, What the Living Do, There Is an Anger That Moves, No Earthly Estate,* and *Oracabessa*) that I consider to be friends. And that have become a part of me.

Back to the wilderness: there are forty days that pass in oblivion. Jesus in isolation. The drama of the encounter with the tempter can mean that the forty days are glossed over quickly. But there's something about them that's worth considering. Did he know that he'd be there for that length of time? Was it a countdown? What did he think would happen? Was he just waiting for the time to feel right for when he'd set off on the way home? What did he do all that time? How was he with his own company? With whom did he speak? Or, perhaps to ask the same question, which of his selves did he speak to? Did any of them answer back?

Isolation became a certain kind of word during the pandemic: *isolate-in-place* I sometimes heard as an imperative. "Isolate" comes from Latin, from *insula*, meaning island. Island yourself. Can we do that? Everything has borders: whether that's internal, or at the shore. Jesus is islanded, a man alone in a place empty of other people. But not empty: there are animals, stars, rocks, whatever he's getting shelter from, insects, and all his other selves. He's visited by those selves, just like many of us are.

It wasn't a devil who slunk up to him, it wasn't a serpent, it wasn't a man in a red-skinned costume complete with horns and a slinky silky tail. It wasn't any of those. It was just one of the versions of himself, inviting him to think about speeding up the process (turn the stones to bread) or ending it all (jump from the temple) or assuming a position of power (bow down and I'll give you all of this). These three things must have been temptations for him: hunger, destruction, influence. Otherwise they wouldn't have been real temptations. A real temptation is when you want it; or half want it, at least. If he hated bread, then bread wouldn't have been of interest. We know this: what wrecks one person doesn't wreck another. What some barely notice is something others barely scrape through.

What's interesting in this strange encounter in isolation is that Jesus's selves engage in a dialogue about literature. Was it his favorite literature? We don't know. Certainly he's been absorbed in it. He turns to a text he knows well — by heart, it seems — in order to host the conversation about the kind of person he would be if he got out of this wilderness. "One does not live by bread alone," he says, to himself, and "Worship the Lord your God; serve only him." Then one of his selves seems to get the trick and quotes the text back to him: "He will command his angels concerning you; to protect you" and "On their hands they will bear you up so that you will not dash your foot against a stone."

Before Jesus closes the argument with a final quote, what we see is that this literature has become a part of him. He knows it so well that he is a rabbinical school in himself, an argument of theologians in a room poring over translations and interpretations. "Who am I to be?" Jesus seems to be asking, as well as "How am I supposed to be who it is I believe I am?" This is a crisis, and what he does not seem able to do is find a way where the text will finally reassure him. Instead, he makes a judgment: he is trying to be bigger than his boots. He is putting God to a test, and he must finish. So, he does. And the others go away.

But he has heard himself in the midst of this awful struggle. Awful because he seems to be alone, because he has no friends around him, at least in Luke and Matthew. The function, however, of the tempter — that shade of Jesus — is that he has had an encounter. And therein lies the value.

Mark's Gospel simply employs two sentences to describe this episode in Jesus's life: "And the Spirit immediately drove him out into the wilderness. He was in the wilderness forty days, tempted by Satan; and he was with the wild beasts; and the angels waited on him." Years ago, I heard it speculated that the wild animals were a literary device meant to give consolation to the Christian community in Rome during a decade when being mauled by lions in the Colosseum for their neighbors' entertainment was a real possibility.

Perhaps this is right — I'll always default to the expertise of scholars who've spent their lives gathering evidence for such speculation. But I hope there's room for other ideas too: the company of animals is a strange one. Watching a wild cat forage for food makes you appreciate the value of hunger. Watching a field mouse carry tiny seeds back underneath a rock honors her instinct of provision. Their teeth, their claws, their fur, their ears always alert for whatever else might be seeking them for food. It's not cute. It's true.

Jesus seems to have been a social man. He is remembered for his friendships, as well as his followers, as well as his capacity to deal well with interruptions most of the time. He spoke to — and praised — people who were used to scorn. Some might have said he was a people person. He was at least interested in people. But he took time alone too: early mornings and all-nighters on mountains and in gardens. And also in wild places. How did he tell his friends about this experience? Somehow someone must have heard. It's a line in Mark, then a longer narrative in both Luke and Matthew. It's not in John. Nobody knows why.

Of course, Jesus's "wrestling with himself" might just be a literary device. But I like to think that he told stories about facing himself, a story that became theologized a little. All there was in the desert was him, some animals, and the other versions of him too. He had to listen. He had to meet. He had to face. He had to question. He had to search for certitude, and in the absence of certitude, he had to choose. It was temporary, this isolation, this islanded self. Soon he was speaking of it, sharing it, telling it, mythologizing it into a tempter with fiery eyes and cloven hooves. The truth is in there too, of course: the things that could threaten to undo him.

What voices do I hear in isolation? What literature do I turn to that shapes the conversation? What do I do? Whom do I tell? What certitude do I search for? What do I do in the collapse of this certitude? What friends do I seek out for conversation in the after? It's strange to note that the sometimes random books you read — or films you watch, or conversations you overhear — might be the ones you turn to during a time of isolation: in a wilderness, in a pandemic, when dizzy in the middle of the night.

A Prayer after Times of Pandemic

God of the Northern Lights,
to you,
a thousand nights
are like one night
and whatever time is
is not time to you.
We are in time, though,
and what happens over years
stays inside our bodies
waiting for a touch,
a story, a tenderness of healing.
Help us help us:
with the time needed for integration;
with the time needed for risk;
with the time for recovery
and honor and trying old things again
and trying new things again too.
Because here, in time,
we seek moments of transcendence
that can remind us of
who we are capable of being.
Amen.

Plenty of Room at the Inn, and Other Stories about Mary

YEARS AGO I WAS THE CELEBRANT at a wedding of dear friends and had put together some stories to tell the congregation. Throughout, one of the brides shouted contradictions from behind me. "That's not how it happened!" she argued through her laughter, "it was a Tuesday, not a Friday!" God almighty. "Stop interrupting the story with the truth!" her mother cried from the congregation. Everyone laughed — it was that kind of service. The bride put the story to rights when she had the microphone. More laughter.

We all know this to be true: everyone remembers things differently. After the death of someone, everyone tells the story of that someone differently. Death isn't even necessary; tell the story of meeting your friend last week, and they'll probably contradict you, adding some detail you'd omitted or — crucially — chosen to gloss over for the purpose of flourish, charm, or cohesion.

How much more is this dynamic seen, then, when it comes to ancient stories, where the possibility of an individual life is so intermeshed with the tectonic plates of theology, redemption, occupation, and cohesion? The seeming singularity of a biblical story — especially when there may only be one telling of that particular sequence — suggests things in a specific order, with clear theological purposes. Well, sometimes. But there's so much space that's needed. It's like the characters need space to turn, space to have a conversation with themselves, space to show you a different version of their own face. To know the way a character's story progresses means we might think we know them, or worse, understand them. We don't. We only know a little.

—◇—

Mary is a character I've been troubled by — and, truth be told, troubled *for* — over many years. Through her eyes, I wondered what it means to own your own life: hers was so caught up in the birth and life and death of her strange son. What would she have felt about herself? What would she have stated as her deepest desire? What would she have wanted? What were her thoughts? What were her senses of failure?

Many know the story of how she's introduced in Luke's Gospel: an angel is sent to her, in Nazareth, and she's described as a "virgin engaged to a man whose name was Joseph." Virgin. Of course, it can be understood simply as *maiden* too. There are stories of virgin births in mythologies from Egypt to China, Greece to Mexico. It's an old plot, and the idea of virgin birth seems to symbolize some inbreaking, an exception to the rule of ordinary conception, that demands attention on the born. In Christian — and in particular I can speak about Catholic — tellings, it seems that virginity has become synonymous with purity. Somehow the forgoing of sex, in the conception of her son, but also in her long-standing sexuality, meant that Mary was purer. I'm a former virgin myself, and purity had very little to do with it. My lack of losing my virginity was driven by opportunity's lack.

Anyway, the angel has visited and has called Mary "highly graced one," which is, in Greek, *kecharitomene*, a particular word that is found nowhere else in the Christian texts, and also a word in a particular tense found nowhere else in the New Testament — or so I read. Nobody else is named in such a way, and, importantly, nobody else is named in the perfect passive participle of Greek that the angel speaks.

Here we remind ourselves that, of course, the angel spoke Aramaic, and that Mary told someone, who told someone, who told someone else, who told someone who could write, who told someone who could translate, who told someone who could write in Greek, who wrote something like what we have today. I'm moved by much in language, but it's also only a signpost.

In the Greek, the implication is that Mary's gracing is something that's confirmed by the angel, not caused. She has already found favor in the eyes of God, it seems. And, again, much is made of this. She's told she'll have a son, and how to name him, and that he will be great, and that he will have a throne given to him by God, a throne from which he'll reign. And as a sign to bear witness to this, too, she's told that she'll find evidence of this by making a visit to her cousin Elizabeth. She gives consent — "let it be with me according to your word" — and then the angel goes, never, it seems, to return again.

What really happened? We don't know. The early Christian writer Origen (he lived from around 185 to 253) refuted a story in one of his writings: a story that suggested Jesus's father was a Roman soldier, a man named Pantera. It's the subject of a lot of historical debate, of course. What interests me is what would happen if we found it to be true. If it were true — and if Jesus knew about it — it'd explain his sometimes-ambivalent relationship to nationalism, as well as give some indication about his lack of shockability in matters sexual. If it were true, it'd be a far more interesting theological story than a miracle: someone born in a relationship marked by anything from scandal to violence is considered to be the incarnation of God.

We have this story, instead. We have Gabriel and Joseph, not Pantera. Gabriel leaves, Joseph's barely in the story, and then Mary leaves too: to go to her cousin's home. She goes "with haste." This isn't a traipse across the countryside in excitement at babies. Luke's Gospel is replete with militarism, and this is occupied territory — soldiers everywhere. Would she have made this trip by day or by night? At dawn or at dusk? How would you decide when would be safest? In the story as told, Mary is a young woman of so-called marriageable age, traveling alone across territory populated by foreign armies. Haste? I'm amazed she didn't race.

In the telling of this story, Mary is carrying cargo that demonstrates an inbreaking of a covenant into a human story. And she goes seeking evidence in the strange pregnancy of her cousin. When she gets to Elizabeth's home, she's greeted with a cry: "Why has this happened to me, that the mother of my Lord comes to me?" It is all ecstatic, and confirmatory, and joyous.

It is also an echo of another story: when the ark of the covenant was being moved by King David at the beginning of his reign, he took it from Kirjath-jearim — a place now named Abu-Ghosh, about eight miles west of Jerusalem. However, one of his men reached out and touched it and was immediately slain. David was unwilling to bring the ark of the covenant to Jerusalem — "How can the ark of the LORD come into my care?" — and instead deposited the ark, for "three months" (2 Sam. 6:11), at the house of Obed-edom the Gittite, a man whose household was blessed because of this sojourn. When David heard that this blessing had come on the house of the Gittite, he went "with rejoicing" to bring the ark back to Jerusalem, and danced before it as part of the ceremony. It's hard to read this text without seeing it as a literary prefigurement for Mary. Somehow, she embodies both David and the ark of the covenant. The threat is all around her, but she's protected, and Elizabeth — in joy, rather than fear — asks how Mary could come to her, and the child in Elizabeth's womb leaps, dances for joy.

The joy of Luke's version of this story is in a peculiar conversation with the sense of threat present in that of Samuel. What is this death doled out by God to the poor man who touched the ark when he shouldn't have? Is this some indication of the protection of Mary's body by God? Would she have told it like that? A feminist reading of this text could suggest that the violation of the integrity of a woman's body brings death for those who dare to violate her. Another reading could suggest that, once again, a woman's body is being used as the house of God, and query whether, if she'd refused, Mary's withheld consent would have been honored. Between these two possible readings lie many stopping points.

—◇—

We know so little about the story of Mary as she would have told it. The theological weight of the story of the visitation makes it hard to sift through to find whatever might have happened in its own raw detail. Some would be content to believe it all happened just as it's narrated. But the story told is always a lens. We translate ourselves for the benefit of narrative, and in honor of a future that hasn't happened yet. There is perspective and literary accompaniment in this story. What seems to remain with us is that a young woman became pregnant and went to an older cousin. Along the way is fear. And, it seems to me, doubt, caution, and the demand for courage.

In those days a decree went out from Emperor Augustus that all the world should be registered. This was the first registration and was taken while Quirinius was governor of Syria. All went to their own towns to be registered. Joseph also went from the town of Nazareth in Galilee to Judea, to the city of David called Bethlehem, because he was descended from the house and family of David. He went to be registered with Mary, to whom he was engaged and who was expecting a child. While they were there, the time came for her to deliver her child. And she gave birth to her firstborn son and wrapped him in bands of cloth, and laid him in a manger, because there was no place for them in the inn.

Read it again, because there is a necessary conflict I wish to introduce. The way we tell Bible stories is often unfaithful to the text. Luke's Gospel — from which much of the story comes — records no animals, no stable, and, most importantly, no inhospitality. Luke, normally so kind and gracious, giving so much time to stories of the marginalized, rushes through the birth of Jesus as if it were of little importance. Joseph and Mary had gone to Bethlehem for the census and:

141

> While they were there, the time came for her to deliver her child. And she gave birth to her firstborn son and wrapped him in bands of cloth, and laid him in a manger, because there was no place for them in the inn.

See? No animals, no inhospitality, no stable.

There is a deeper story here, one of kind hospitality. And it hinges upon the word used for "inn."

When we hear the word "inn," we tend to think of a resting house, with an owner, and rooms, kind of like a medieval hostel where you could rest your horses and get a room for a night. In biblical Greek there are two words for inn — *kataluma* and *pandocheion*. Luke uses both words for inn throughout his gospel. When — later in the text — he invents a story about a mobbed man who was helped by a Samaritan, he uses the word *pandocheion*, which does indeed translate as a resting house, with an owner and rooms.

But he does not use that word in the nativity story.

When the family finds out there is no place in the "inn," the word used is *kataluma*. A *kataluma* was a different thing altogether. Most people of the time lived in a one-room structure. In that room there was space for living and sleeping, a hearth perhaps. Animals, if you had them, were brought in for the night to that same space — for protection and also because of the warmth they'd give. Those houses lucky enough to have a *kataluma* had an additional upper room. This room, the *kataluma*, the upper room, could be rented out, like the ancient world's equivalent of Airbnb.

Joseph and Mary, arriving in Bethlehem, could not find a *kataluma*. They were in Bethlehem because that's where Joseph's kinsfolk were. So, they had the baby and laid him in the manger. The manger would have been where mangers always were: in the living space of a family, a family who made room for Joseph, Mary, and Jesus in their own home. Presumably they were relatives of Joseph.

This is more ordinary, less dramatic. And, importantly, this reading is much less offensive to Jews who are aghast at tellings of the nativity story that imply that anyone would turn away any woman — whether kinsfolk or not — in the last moments of pregnancy.

Luke's story of *kataluma* continues. At the end of the gospel, Jesus and his friends meet for a meal — a last supper — and this time, he makes it to the *kataluma*. At this stage of most translations, the word is more accurately translated as being akin to "an upper room."

—◇—

The way we tell the story tells so much. Stars and angels and joy and delight. Also, inhospitality, cruelty, unintended insult, and limitation. We must always be attentive to the edges of our own storytelling. Attractive as it may be to children, lodged as it may be in the illustrations on religious Christmas cards, it is simply incorrect to think that Mary and Joseph were forced into a stable. They found shelter in the kindness of people, presumably Joseph's kin, in his traditional homeland of Bethlehem. This kindness was so ordinary, so expected, so taken for granted that Luke, the gentle evangelist, did not even make mention of the family whose home was used for what we consider to be the birthing of a godchild to confused parents.

The telling of a particular story can make many things possible.

To tell the story in one way implies something about the character of people in Bethlehem at the time — that they would send a woman to a stable to give birth. It is necessary to introduce conflict into received readings of this story: by doing that, we might realize that every moment of human encounter, every small demonstration of hospitality, carries within it the possibility for incarnation. We can see that human touch, the actual touching of flesh and flesh, is in itself sacred. We can also see that religion at its best can communicate an honor for the ordinary, the everyday, the unremarkable — can find something remarkable in the midst of this parochial normality.

Mary and Joseph are depicted as devout, bringing the child up to the temple for a blessing at his circumcision. There they meet Simeon and Anna, older people who deliver strange messages to her. The Scottish liturgist and musician John Bell often points out how the story of Mary seems to be populated with older people: Elizabeth, the unnamed women at the house where Jesus was born, Simeon, Anna.

> Then Simeon blessed them and said to his mother Mary, "This child is destined for the falling and the rising of many in Israel, and to be a sign that will be opposed so that the inner thoughts of many will be revealed — and a sword will pierce your own soul too."

Maybe Mary already knew this; maybe the sword had already gone in, in whatever version of the story she'd lived through and survived. The conflict at the heart of these stories is about occupation and politics. It is also about one person's story being told against a backdrop of a national story. What interests me in trying to revisit the story now is that I want there to be space around her, in order for multiple possibilities to exist: she wanted everything to be different; or she was delighted to be part of the resistance to Rome; she was thrilled at the break from tradition; she was devastated; she wanted a more straightforward story of parenthood; or she embraced the breaking with tradition; she threw herself into the commitment of her marriage to Joseph with joy; she went there for protection. Who knows? We don't. What helps is space.

I Came to Bring Fire to the Earth:
Toward a Spirituality of Conflict

"I CAME TO BRING FIRE TO THE EARTH, and how I wish it were already kindled! I have a baptism with which to be baptized, and what stress I am under until it is completed! Do you think that I have come to bring peace to the earth? No, I tell you, but rather division! From now on five in one household will be divided, three against two and two against three; they will be divided:

father against son
    and son against father,
mother against daughter
    and daughter against mother,
mother-in-law against her daughter-in-law
    and daughter-in-law against
        mother-in-law."

He also said to the crowds, "When you see a cloud rising in the west, you immediately say, 'It is going to rain'; and so it happens. And when you see the south wind blowing, you say, 'There will be scorching heat'; and it happens. You hypocrites! You know how to interpret the appearance of earth and sky, but why do you not know how to interpret the present time?"

(Luke 12:49–56)

Living and working in a wide variety of faith contexts over the years has revealed to me how it is that religion, culture, power, gender, personality, consequence, money, threat, and privilege all overlap when it comes to performing conflict. I say *performing* because that is often what happens. Something is happening, and our lives become the stage upon which that something is acted out. Others are co-opted into our performance, and the more vital the conflict is and feels, the more we can be both actor and director. Often, we are the audience too: although it can take a long time to notice what's happening on the stage of our lives.

"I came to bring fire to the earth," Jesus says, and then goes on to fantasize about division: three against two and two against three. The Jesus of this text includes conflict as a possible consequence to faithfulness. It may not feel like a comforting reading, but there are strange consolations to be found in it, especially for anyone whose chosen faithfulness involves complicated consequences.

Before going on, it's a useful thing — as always — to reflect on your own general feelings about conflict. Obviously each circumstance differs, but it's even worthwhile doing a broad brush-strokes reflection: When it comes to conflict, do you embrace it? Is that easy? Or awkward? Or do you tend to avoid it? Are you at ease in times when your wishes and those of another differ? When such differences occur, do you seek to assert your point of view? Do you tend to seek compromises or middle ground? Do you tend to acquiesce?

Also: What are the feelings that accompany your general responses to situations of conflict? Does it cause hope in you, the hope of the electricity of cocreating and collaborating? Or does it cause anxiety?

In a broad sense, conflict can be assessed along the axes of cooperation and competition: Do you assent or assert? Everyone has multiple modes, and these are dependent on personality, circumstance, society, time, and power. For instance, a naturally assertive person may find themselves acquiescing to a boss who has demonstrated that they have a tendency to fire people who stand up to them. Or, a naturally accommodating person may stress their point in a situation of conflict where justice needs to be served.

As depicted in the gospels, Jesus of Nazareth is consistently unafraid of conflict. He doesn't pursue it, but he does not shy away from it. Our text from Luke is often misunderstood to imply that followers of the gospel should seek out conflict, but it doesn't say that. Instead, it's one attempt to share his own disposition toward conflict with his disciples.

The words attributed to Jesus by Luke are interestingly elemental: fire, water, and wind are all mentioned. As are origins: "I came to bring . . ." The broader personality of Jesus is being established by his priorities, his divine purpose. He speaks of fire — not of destruction, but of initiation: "I have a baptism with which to be . . ." He speaks about divisions within family units before urging his followers to see the signs of the times the same way they would read the weather systems approaching them.

In a sense, this text can be understood as a coaching session to reluctant disciples, encouraging them not to be afraid of tensions within their close-knit units. To have an opinion is to care deeply for something, and this opinion may cause tensions between you and those with whom you disagree. Tension — another way of saying conflict — is not a terror. It is also not the end of the world. It invites a person to ask themselves, "Do I really believe this? What happens when those I love think differently?"

If your only mode of operation is keeping the peace, maintaining the appearance of a lack of tension within a close-knit unit, then this text is for you. It provokes. It upsets. It cajoles. It asks, "What do you stand for if you'll change your mind just so as to keep the facade of peace?" Given that the early Christians were constantly in tension with each other about big questions — gentile inclusion in a religious movement begun by Jews; circumcision; the crisis of death; money; loyalty to political powers — the inclusion of this text asks for attention.

What *is* your spirituality during times of conflict? What informs it? How do you pursue information? How do you practice disagreement with those you love? How do your loving relationships hold — or withhold — existing tensions? And how do you practice spirituality in the conflicts you have with yourself?

Conflict is not an end in itself; this is important to remember, especially for those who are naturally at ease in conflict. Most congregations and communities have some people who find it easy to use a time of conflict to assert what they want, perhaps because of a natural disposition to enjoy conflict — or at least not be frightened by it. This behavior is also often supported by societal norms. Depending on where you live, your age, race, gender, economic, or educational status can make your assertions more likely to be accepted no matter their merits. So it is important to remember that conflict is not an end in itself.

And this brings us back to the opening words of Luke's text: "I came . . . ," Luke has Jesus say, ". . . to bring fire on the earth" and to link that fire with baptism. What is the aim in any situation of conflict? If it is simply to *win*, then it is likely to eventually be fruitless. Conflict must seek some other purpose than its own propagation, its own victory. It must be in the service of creation: of a just society, of a more hopeful present, of a more flourishing world, of a safer environment, of a more sustainable world, of a richer communion.

A Prayer for Times of Conflict

Fiery Jesus, you were seized

with a sense of purpose
that caused you to pursue what you saw was
    right.
When we do this
help us light the way
and burn a little too
so that we might bear what it is we propose,
if we haven't already.
Amen.

Hold Yourself Together and
Pull Yourself Apart

> In a time of desolation do not make a
> life-changing decision and do not go
> back on a decision made during a time
> of consolation. Remember the times
> of consolation.
>
> — Ignatius of Loyola

Remember that this has passed before
and that there will be more days
of plenty . . . eventually.

Pay attention to your feelings
keep those feelings sharp.
Try to hold yourself together
and pull yourself apart.
Keep your eyes on the prize
that you might never gain.

Don't ignore whatever pain is blooming
like a flower that you never planted.
Occupy your hands with kindness.
Remember you can see, even though this unseeing
is remarkable.

From *Readings from the Book of Exile*. Canterbury Press, 2012.
Used with permission.

Mark the places that you're feeling
mark the spaces where you're needing held
mark the evenings that are dark
and mark the afternoon of coping.

Mark the morning that you waken
finding mourning has been taken
to a different part of heartland.

Remember what has passed before.
Pour your body like the sacramental wine
pour your blood with loving.

Acknowledgments

THIS BOOK HAS BEEN a collaboration between the Church of the Heavenly Rest and Pádraig Ó Tuama, who has become an anchor in our rhythms of life and prayer at the church.

Parishioner Elizabeth Boe introduced me to Pádraig's work years ago, and I subsequently carried *Daily Prayer with the Corrymeela Community* — the prayer book he wrote while leader of Ireland's oldest peace and reconciliation organization — around the world with me. His prayer for courage found in those pages has been a personal lodestar: "We bear witness to our faith, knowing that we are called to live lives of courage, love, and reconciliation in the ordinary and extraordinary moments of each day."

We were delighted to invite Pádraig to join Church of the Heavenly Rest as our first artist-in-residence in 2020 — a plan changed dramatically by the Covid-19 pandemic. Travel restrictions meant that early on he joined us remotely from Ireland, often late at night his time. Pádraig led retreats and Bible study online; he taught us how to write prayers.

It was an amazing experience, full of generative conversations and silences. And during that time, Pádraig also wrote a devotional book for our community centered on a daily rhythm of readings and prayers. It's been a great challenge and comfort to our parish, and we're honored to now share these prayers with a much broader community.

I'm incredibly grateful to Pádraig Ó Tuama for his time with us. Anne Marie Witchger, Elizabeth Boe, Lucy Appert, Tim Lively, Anne Rademacher, Adam MacDonald, Cindy Stravers, and Lucas Thorpe provided key support and guidance through his residency — both online and when he was able to join us in New York City. Lucas directed publication of this book with support from Marjorie McKittrick, Edith Webster Freed, and Vi Lynk. It's a joy to work with this talented group of people.

We also thank Lisa Ann Cockrel and the whole team at Eerdmans for guiding us through the publication process.

Just as Pádraig's work has become an anchor at Church of the Heavenly Rest, my hope is that this devotional book will be a steadfast companion in the prayer lives of our neighbors here on the Upper East Side of Manhattan, across the United States, and around the world. May this book be a blessing in your life and your own practice of *being here*, being present to the sacred moments in your own life wherever you live.

The Right Reverend Matthew Foster Heyd
Spring 2023